GOOD APPLE
&
WONDERFUL WORD GAMES

by

Mary & David Dunning

Illustrated by Mary & David Dunning

Cover by Nancee Volpe
Assisted by Tom Sjoerdsma

Copyright © Good Apple, Inc., 1981

ISBN No. 0-86653-053-3

Printing No. 987654321

The purchase of this book entitles the buyer to duplicate the activity pages as need-ed, for use by students in the buyer's classroom. Permission for any other use must be granted by Good Apple, Inc.

GOOD APPLE, INC.
BOX 299
CARTHAGE, IL 62321

All rights reserved. Printed in the USA
by Crest Litho, Inc., Albany, NY

Table of Contents

Table of Contents (cont'd.)

Introduction

We created these activity pages for three reasons:

1) To encourage creativity, one of our most valuable skills,

2) To make learning fun, since we all learn more from things we enjoy,

3) To intrigue children with the significance of words, and enhance their lifelong process of communication.

CELEBRATE LIFE!

CREATE,

ENJOY,

COMMUNICATE,

& LEARN!

THAT'S THE REASON WE ARE ALL HERE.

WITH LOVE,
MARY & DAVE

The Power of Words

The words we use are very important. What we send out, we get back. The words we use to communicate with others return to us. If there is a part of our world we want to change, we can take a giant step by changing the way we talk about it. For example, if we are interested in happy, pleasant relationships, are we using happy, pleasant words? This chapter has some activities which sample a few of the ways words affect us. Along with practice in word usage and mental exercise, students have an opportunity to get a better understanding of the consequences of their words. Developing a feel for the close relationship between the words we speak and the way others react to us is an extremely valuable process for us all, at any age or level.

WORDS

...others to cheer up

Words I say to

Places we find words...

Special words...

Strange or funny words I know...

Words that make me happy...

The WORD WIZARD who did this is

I use words with care because ___

I AM A WORD WIZARD!

ME!

I learn new words best when ___

Words that I love to hear...

Words that scare me...

Things we can learn from a dictionary

These words always cause a strong reaction...

Words are important because ___

2

Powerful Words

When we hear some words we feel good, happy, proud, and self-confident; when we hear others we may feel upset, hurt, angry or unsure of ourselves. It is important to learn which words trigger which reactions. Think about personal experiences you've had and list words to which you react strongly. Sharing your completed lists is an opportunity to learn about words. Which words do many of us like and dislike? How can you use this information to make your life work better?

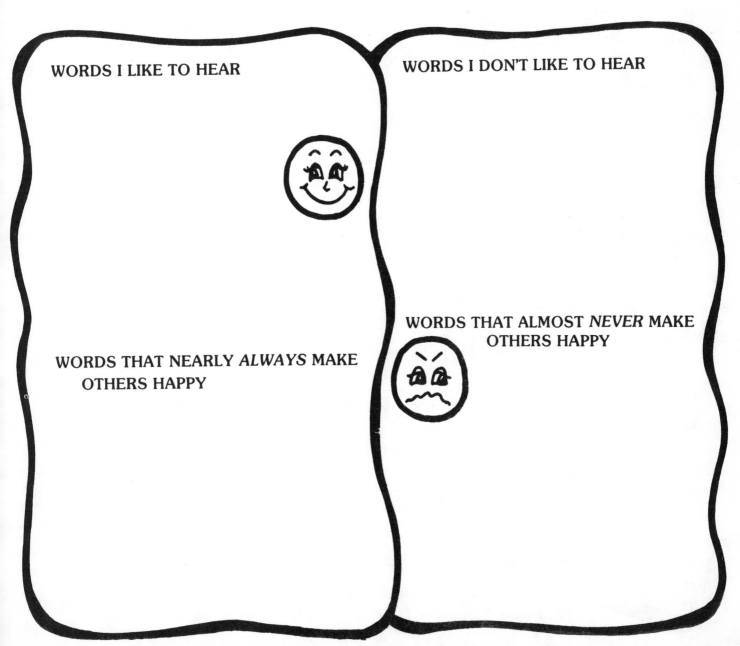

WORDS I LIKE TO HEAR

WORDS I DON'T LIKE TO HEAR

WORDS THAT ALMOST *NEVER* MAKE OTHERS HAPPY

WORDS THAT NEARLY *ALWAYS* MAKE OTHERS HAPPY

When we pay attention to our feelings, we have a better understanding of what we are experiencing. We can then choose whether or not we want to change. To become more aware of your feelings, make an alphabetical list of words that describe emotions.

A _____

B _____

C _____

D _____

E _____

F _____

G _____

H _____

I _____

J,K _____

L _____

M _____

N,O _____

P _____

Q _____

R _____

S _____

T _____

U _____

V,W _____

X,Y,Z _____

HAPPY, SAD or PEACEFUL

See if you can put each of the 42 words below into the correct category. Use the dictionary if you need help.

glad	relaxed	upset	lonely	excited	cheerful
sorrowful	tranquil	joyful	gloomy	still	melancholy
unruffled	bright	quiet	calm	delighted	unhappy
spiritless	inspired	mild	pleased	settled	merry
restful	troubled	elated	discouraged	blissful	composed
ecstatic	content	satisfied	dreary	jolly	miserable
disheartened	pensive	jubilant	untroubled	solemn	gentle

Happy

_____
_____
_____
_____
_____
_____
_____
_____
_____
_____
_____
_____
_____
_____

Sad

_____
_____
_____
_____
_____
_____
_____
_____
_____
_____
_____
_____
_____
_____

Peaceful

_____
_____
_____
_____
_____
_____
_____
_____
_____
_____
_____
_____
_____
_____

5

ALL ABOUT ME

Design a T-shirt with words which describe *YOU*, either now or the way you want to be.

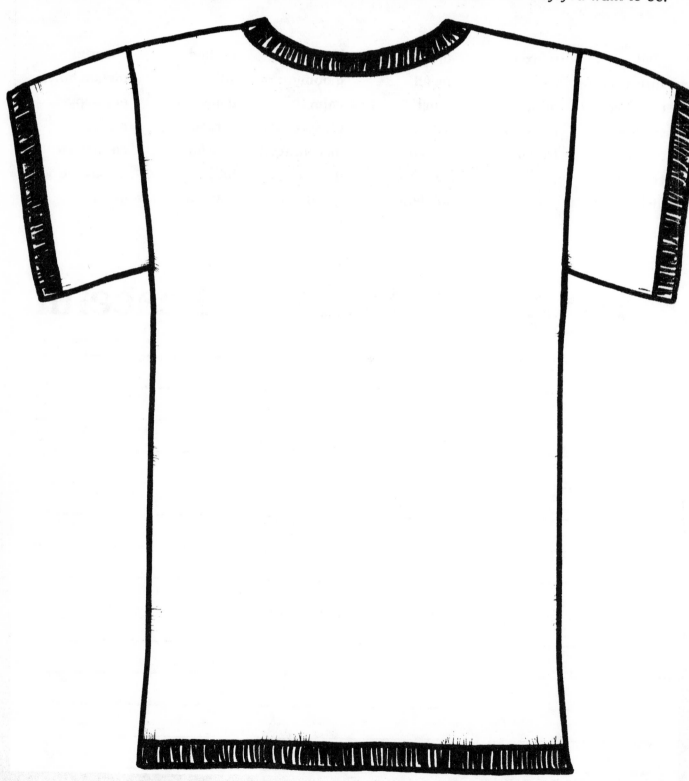

Persuasive Words

PERSUASIVE words are words that tempt and influence us. They are used in many places to invite us to buy things, visit places, vote for people, contribute money to causes and choose one option over another. Persuasive words tend to encourage us to accept someone else's ideas instead of forming our own. LOOK and LISTEN carefully for 24 hours. Notice your friends, your parents, the TV, newspapers, magazines, store windows, etc., then use this page to make a collage of persuasive words and phrases. You can cut them out of magazines, ads, junk mail or newspapers. You can also write them on different sizes and colors of paper to make an interesting design. This activity will make you more aware of persuasive advertising techniques we come in contact with every day.

Mental Exercising

A great way to exercise your brain is to stretch beyond where you usually stop. See how many words you can think of that fit these categories. Be sure to use your imagination!

SCORING each category: 1-6 words = 1 point each, 8-14 = 2 points each, 16-26 = 3 points, 24 or more = 4 points.

1-8 points = OK, 10-22 = Good, 24-30 = Very Good, 32 or more = Excellent

---

8 WORDS THAT *SOUND* LIKE WHAT THEY DESCRIBE (such as OOZE)

1. _____ 9. _____
2. _____ 10. _____
3. _____ 11. _____
4. _____ 12. _____
5. _____ 13. _____
6. _____ 14. _____
7. _____ 15. _____
8. _____ 16. _____

8 WORDS THAT TELL HOW SOMETHING FEELS TO THE *TOUCH* (such as SMOOTH)

1. _____ 9. _____
2. _____ 10. _____
3. _____ 11. _____
4. _____ 12. _____
5. _____ 13. _____
6. _____ 14. _____
7. _____ 15. _____
8. _____ 16. _____

8 WORDS DESCRIBING THINGS MOST PEOPLE *REACT TO* VERY STRONGLY (such as WAR)

1. _____ 9. _____
2. _____ 10. _____
3. _____ 11. _____
4. _____ 12. _____
5. _____ 13. _____
6. _____ 14. _____
7. _____ 15. _____
8. _____ 16. _____

8 WORDS THAT MEAN THE SAME, OR NEARLY THE SAME, AS *SAID* (such as EXPLAINED)

1. _____ 9. _____
2. _____ 10. _____
3. _____ 11. _____
4. _____ 12. _____
5. _____ 13. _____
6. _____ 14. _____
7. _____ 15. _____
8. _____ 16. _____

Creativity

Creativity is one of our most precious resources. Fortunately, the supply is limitless! The more we use it, the more we have. It's also FUN to use this illusive mental process, and the results of regular practice are astounding.

The four basic creative abilities are FLUENCY (generating a free flow of many thoughts, items, or options), FLEXIBILITY (looking at things differently, finding other angles), ORIGINALITY (coming up with the unusual and ingenious idea), and ELABORATION (expanding ideas, and adding details). It is essential to the development of these abilities that we provide time in our classrooms when creativity is appropriate and rewarded. This chapter has a few ideas to use in your classroom to encourage creativity with words.

The more ideas we come up with, the more clever and unique our responses tend to be. With this in mind, it is important to allow a flow of ideas without criticism or censure. Encourage as many responses as possible, the wilder, the better! While we may find it challenging at times to handle divergent thinkers (for example, the student who maintains that symmetry and geometry are types of trees, the child who has seven OTHER ways to do things, and the child who is a humorous adlibber), the process they are using is the same one that leads to inventions and turns problems into solutions.

BRAINSTORMING

Brainstorming is a creative technique that can be used with all age groups and for any subject matter. It is thinking up as many ideas as possible on a given topic. Quantity is the main result, and you'll be pleased with the increasing productivity from your class with each activity. The greater the number of responses, the greater the quality, flexibility and originality. Brainstorming can

      make learning fun,

          put basic skills to use,

              develop thinking and listening skills,

                  increase vocabulary,

                     exercise the imagination,

                        allow all students to be successful,

                           and encourage idea sharing!

You can begin with large group activities and record responses to open-ended questions on the chalkboard. Encourage ALL responses without judging them verbally or nonverbally. Challenge the group to keep thinking past the usual point of "I can't think of anything else." Discuss how many ideas they came up with, what good ideas they have, and which are the most unusual in your group.

After a few group experiences, have students list individually on paper (with or without time limit). Briefly share the number of ideas and the most original ones. Then repeat the activity in groups of two or three, with one person recording. Everyone now has something to contribute, and he will piggy-back on the ideas of others. Process this activity in the same way as the large group exercise. Besides increasing fluency, this is a great lesson in the value of synergy. The group lists will usually be longer than individual ones, given an equal amount of time and concentration.

Display your brainstorming results often, on adding machine tape, butcher paper, etc., so students can read the lists, add to their vocabulary, and see their great progress.

Here are some sample brainstorming patterns. (For more specific examples, see the Graffiti pages.)

HOW MANY _____ CAN YOU LIST? HOW MANY WAYS CAN YOU ...? WHAT MIGHT HAPPEN IF ...? HOW CAN WE CHANGE _____? HOW ELSE COULD WE ...? HOW WOULD THINGS BE DIFFERENT IF ... ? WHAT WOULD _____ _____ BE LIKE IF IT WERE MODIFIED (MADE LARGER, SMALLER, REVERSED, COMBINED)?

How many ways can YOU fit this fun, creative thinking technique into your classroom?

GRAFFITI

Graffiti posters offer a channel for making words and creativity a daily part of your classroom. Place questions around your room on butcher paper covering the door, on table tops, on a section of your chalkboard, etc. This idea can be used effectively to reinforce lessons, enrich subject areas, share ideas, and encourage creative thinking and writing. This is a nonthreatening way for students to express themselves, and for you to find out more about how they think and feel.

You can focus on general subjects or specific questions that spark an abundance of responses. Let your students react in writing throughout the week, using only acceptable language and no names. Change your posters often - as they become filled up, when they are outdated, or if one doesn't seem to work well. Dress up your graffiti space with colorful letters, drawings that relate, magazine pictures, etc.

The ideas which follow are suggestions intended to help you and your students become more fluent, more thoine pictures, etc.

The ideas which follow are suggestions intended to help you and your students become more fluent, more thoughtful and more creative.

WHAT ARE YOUR FAVORITE ...?

songs, foods, pets, noises, sports, expressions, vegetables, places, clothes...

HOW MANY WORDS CAN YOU LIST THAT ...?

express emotions
are adjectives, verbs, etc.
have a double letter B (L, T, D, R, S, etc.)
end in E (ED, ING, TE, TION, SHIP, etc.)
describe a friend, a haunted house, a baseball game, a vacation, a good grade, our room...

sound like what they mean
start with an A, a B, a C...
start with S and end with E
start with the prefix RE...

HOW MANY THINGS DO YOU ASSOCIATE WITH...?

spring
the beach
school
ice-cream cones
bare feet
parents
bicycles
water

TV
McDonalds
friends
sports
corn on the cob
plants
sunny days
laughter

blue jeans
parades
weekends
birds
your sister/brother
food
kangaroos
outer space

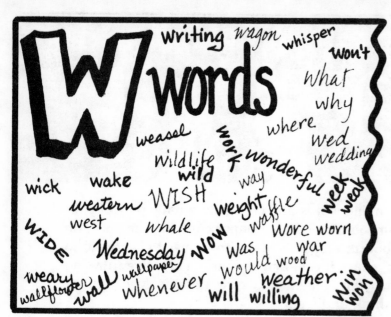

W words

writing wagon whisper won't
What why where Wed wedding
weasel work wonderful
wildlife wild
wick wake way weak
western WISH weight week
west whale WOW waffle
WIDE Wednesday wore worn
weary was war
wallflower would wood
wall wallpaper whenever weather Win won
will willing

HOW MANY THINGS CAN YOU FIND IN A (N)...?

attic	toolbox
garage	old trunk
desk drawer	flower bed
city block	kitchen cupboard
office	gym
school	toy box
restaurant	spaceship

LIST DIFFERENT KINDS OF....

animals	toys
trees	flowers
feelings	colors
tools	cities
insects	countries
transportation	vegetables
cars	fruits
fish	reptiles

LIST THINGS THAT ARE...

ticklish	shiny
sticky	cool
frightening	tiny
delicious	foamy
bitter	bumpy
sweet	icy
furry	slippery
rough	light
beautiful	warm
weird	fragile
sensitive	very heavy
round	wet
sharp	mysterious
silly	comfortable

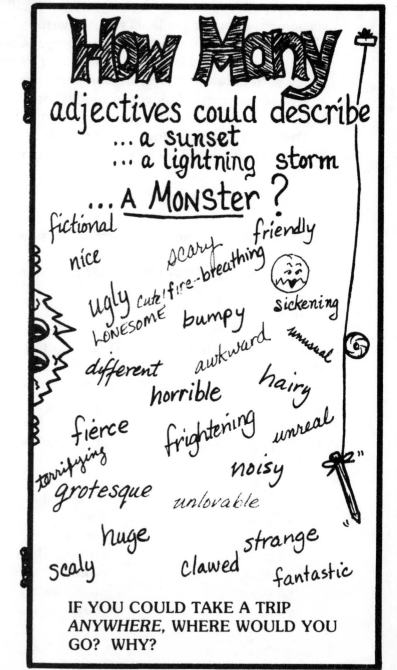

How Many

adjectives could describe
...a sunset
...a lightning storm
...A Monster?

fictional
nice scary friendly
ugly cute! fire-breathing
LONESOME bumpy sickening
different awkward unusual
horrible hairy
fierce frightening unreal
terrifying noisy
grotesque unlovable
huge strange
scaly clawed fantastic

IF YOU COULD TAKE A TRIP *ANYWHERE*, WHERE WOULD YOU GO? WHY?

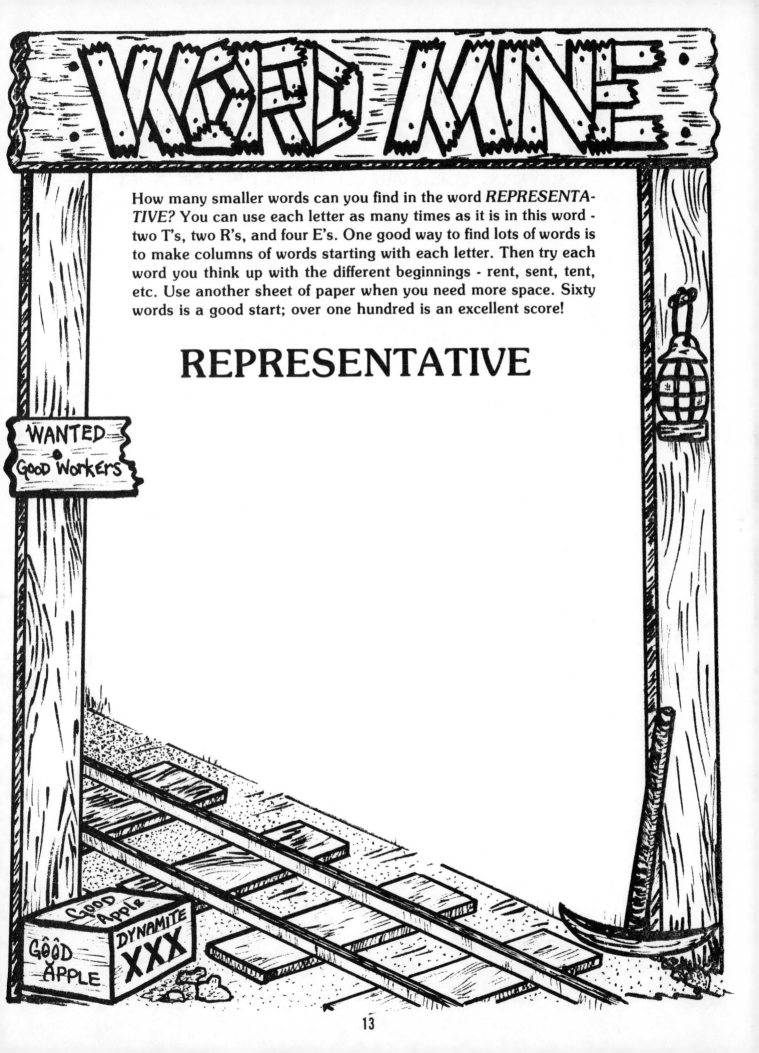

WORD MINE

How many smaller words can you find in the word *REPRESENTATIVE?* You can use each letter as many times as it is in this word - two T's, two R's, and four E's. One good way to find lots of words is to make columns of words starting with each letter. Then try each word you think up with the different beginnings - rent, sent, tent, etc. Use another sheet of paper when you need more space. Sixty words is a good start; over one hundred is an excellent score!

REPRESENTATIVE

WANTED
Good Workers

GOOD
APPLE
GOOD
Apple
DYNAMITE
XXX

HOW MANY WORDS CAN YOU FIND IN THE LETTERS IN *PALINDROME?*

A palindrome is a word or sentence which reads the same way backward or forward. (madam)

Eighty is a good score; over one hundred is excellent.

PALINDROME

WORD BOXES

Put your creativity and knowledge of words to work filling in the Word Boxes below with words that fit in the spaces. Pretend you are a crossword puzzle writer and you are on the first step of a new puzzle.

WORD BOXES

Complete these Words Boxes by thinking of words that will fit in the spaces.

16

How Many Words

CAN YOU THINK OF THAT START WITH
Th?

25 - Fair   35 - Good   50 - Very Good   70 plus - Excellent

17

How Many Words

Do You Know St That start with ?

NOW MAKE A LIST WITH "STR" ANYWHERE IN THE WORD...in*str*ument.

1 point for each ST word; 2 points for each STR word;
3 points for any word with 7 or more letters.

35 - OK
50 - Good

65 - Very Good
85 plus - Excellent

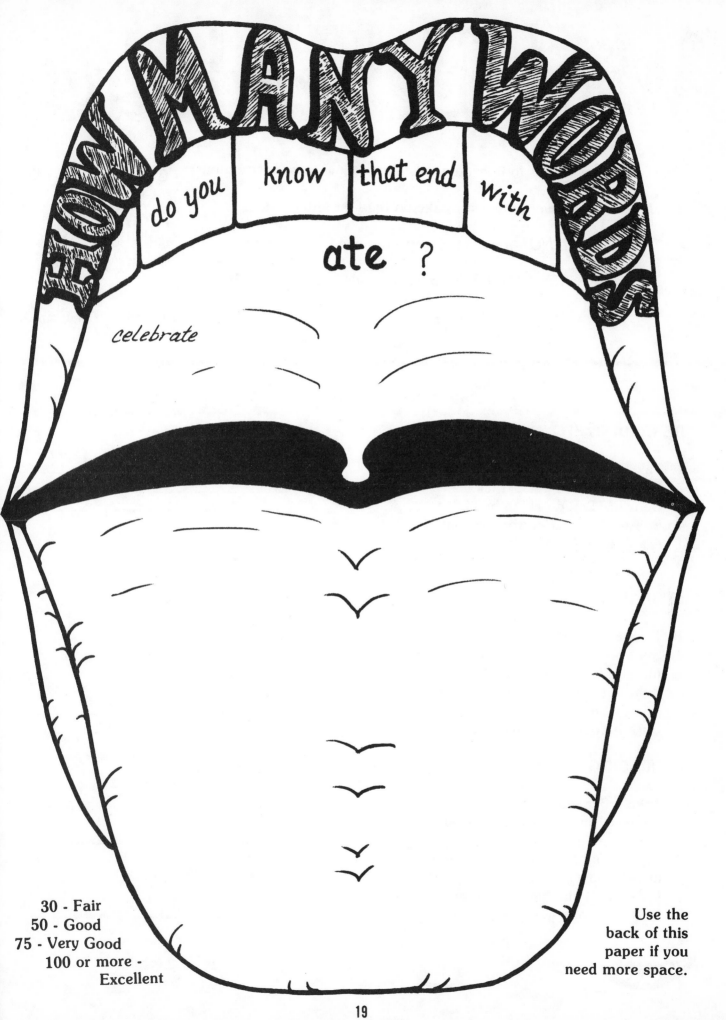

HOW MANY WORDS

do you know that end with

ate ?

celebrate

30 - Fair
50 - Good
75 - Very Good
100 or more -
Excellent

Use the
back of this
paper if you
need more space.

19

Word Beheadings

You need no weapons to behead words! Just follow these instructions:

BEHEADING   a word means to take off the first letter.

CURTAILING   a word means to remove the last letter.

SUBTRACTING   means to take away one of the letters.

TRANSPOSING   means to rearrange the letters to make a new word.

BEHEADING #1

1. Take a five letter word for "path."
2. Behead #1 and get a track.
3. Behead #2 and get "to be ill."
4. Subtract one letter from #3 and get Alan's nickname.
5. Curtail #4 and get one.

BEHEADING #2

1. Take a five letter word for "combat."
2. Subtract one letter and transpose #1 to get a birthday present.
3. Subtract one letter from #2 to get a slang word for "get out."
4. Curtail #3 and get an enlisted man.

BEHEADING #3

1. Take a five letter word for "gravy."
2. Subtract one letter and transpose to get a box.
3. Curtail and transpose #2 to get an insect's pouch.
4. Behead #3 and get alternating current.
5. Curtail #4 and get a beginning.

More Word Beheadings

BEHEADING #4

1. Take a six letter word for "messiah" or one who saves.
2. Subtract one letter and get "taste."
3. Subtract one letter from #2 and transpose to get paddles.
4. Behead and transpose #3 to abbreviate Sons of the American Revolution.
5. Curtail and transpose #4 and get "so far."

_____
_____
_____
_____
_____

BEHEADING #5

1. Start with a five letter word for our planet.
2. Behead and transpose #1 to find "there's gold in them_____ hills!"
3. Subtract one letter from #2 and get pitch.
4. Curtail and transpose #3 and get "where it's_____."
5. Behead #4 and get a shirt.

_____
_____
_____
_____
_____

BEHEADING #6

1. Take a six letter word meaning "attorney."
2. Subtract one letter from #1 and get a single thickness.
3. Subtract one letter and transpose #2 and get actual.
4. Curtail and transpose to get something you hear with.
5. Behead and transpose #4 to get the Egyptian sun god.

_____
_____
_____
_____
_____

Try making up some word beheadings for your friends to work!

Slide-o-Rama

Slide each column of letters up and down independently to make as many different four letter words as you can. Use another piece of paper if you need more room. Thirty words is fair; forty-five is good; and over seventy is excellent.

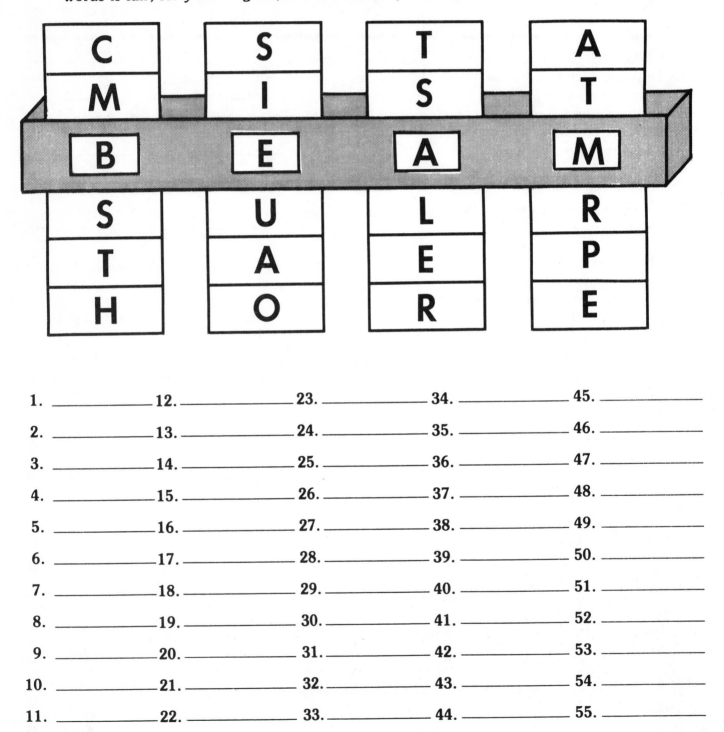

1. _____ 12. _____ 23. _____ 34. _____ 45. _____
2. _____ 13. _____ 24. _____ 35. _____ 46. _____
3. _____ 14. _____ 25. _____ 36. _____ 47. _____
4. _____ 15. _____ 26. _____ 37. _____ 48. _____
5. _____ 16. _____ 27. _____ 38. _____ 49. _____
6. _____ 17. _____ 28. _____ 39. _____ 50. _____
7. _____ 18. _____ 29. _____ 40. _____ 51. _____
8. _____ 19. _____ 30. _____ 41. _____ 52. _____
9. _____ 20. _____ 31. _____ 42. _____ 53. _____
10. _____ 21. _____ 32. _____ 43. _____ 54. _____
11. _____ 22. _____ 33. _____ 44. _____ 55. _____

Word Trees

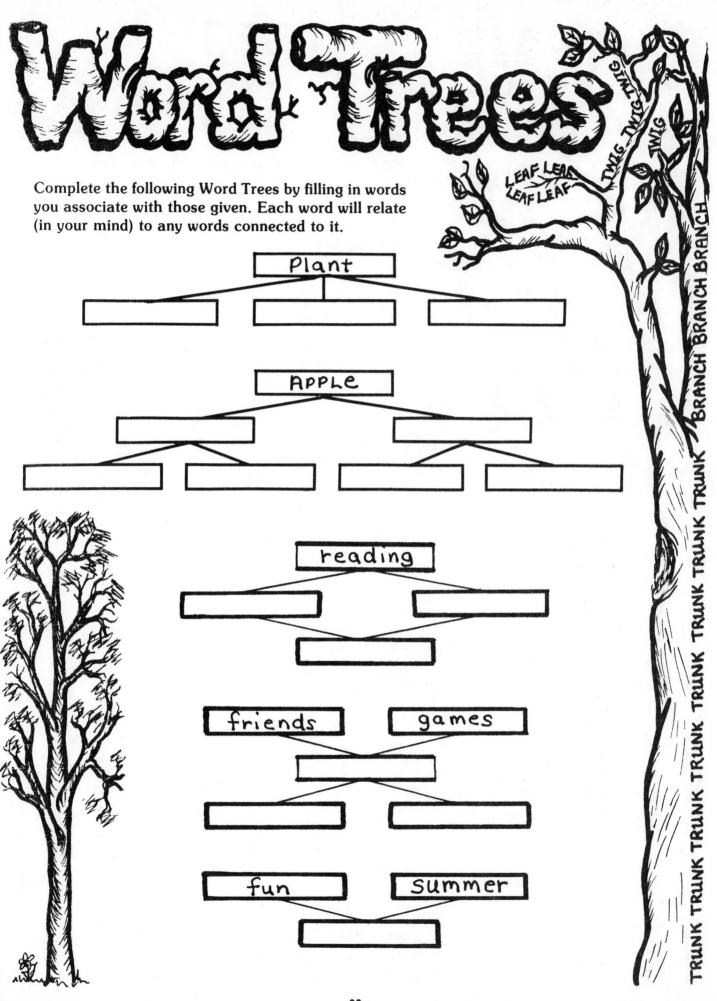

Complete the following Word Trees by filling in words you associate with those given. Each word will relate (in your mind) to any words connected to it.

Plant

Apple

reading

friends   games

fun   summer

Word Trees

What words can you think of to complete these Word Trees?

LOVE

TELEVISION

WATER

24

Word Parts

This chapter focuses on some activities with syllables, prefixes, suffixes, word building, compounds and rhyming words. The purpose of these work sheets is to strengthen the ability of your students to combine, create and use word parts flexibly. Another easy, successful way to call attention to parts of words is to have a graffiti board section of your chalkboard where students can write responses to different topics each day. Some sample topics: "How many words do you know that start with the letter(s)_____?" "How many words can we make with the prefix RE (back, over again)?" "Words which contain the root DUC or DUCT (lead)..." "How many words can we list that end with the suffix IST (one who)?" The possibilities are limitless for devising games and activities to involve children in fun word play.

Heads & Tails

Here is a chance to exercise your vocabulary and stretch your word power. Fill in as many lines as you can with words that start or end with the letters given. Have fun and enjoy the activity! Use the back if you need more room.

t_____	r_____	_____n	_____g
t_____	r_____	_____n	_____g
t_____	r_____	_____n	_____g
t_____	r_____	_____n	_____g
t_____	r_____	_____n	_____g
t_____	r_____	_____n	_____g
t_____	r_____	_____n	_____g
t_____	r_____	_____n	_____g
t_____	r_____	_____n	_____g
t_____	r_____	_____n	_____g
t_____	r_____	_____n	_____g
t_____	r_____	_____n	_____g
t_____	r_____	_____n	_____g
t_____	r_____	_____n	_____g
t_____	r_____	_____n	_____g
t_____	r_____	_____n	_____g
t_____	r_____	_____n	_____g
t_____	r_____	_____n	_____g

When you're done, share your list with your classmates. Who wrote the most words?
Did you think up words no one else listed?

Heads & Tails

Fill in as many words as you can think of that fit the beginning and ending letters given below. Take time to think before you write.

p_____	_____e	m_____r	b_____t
p_____	_____e	m_____r	b_____t
p_____	_____e	m_____r	b_____t
p_____	_____e	m_____r	b_____t
p_____	_____e	m_____r	b_____t
p_____	_____e s	p_____l	_____d
p_____	_____e s	p_____l	_____d
p_____	_____e s	p_____l	_____d
p_____	_____e s	p_____l	_____d
p_____	_____e s	p_____l	_____d
p_____	_____e c	n_____r	_____g
p_____	_____e c	n_____r	_____g
p_____	_____e c	n_____r	_____g
p_____	_____e c	n_____r	_____g
p_____	_____e c	n_____r	_____g
p_____	_____e t	e_____w	_____t
p_____	_____e t	e_____w	_____t
p_____	_____e t	e_____w	_____t
p_____	_____e t	e_____w	_____t
p_____	_____e t	e_____w	_____t

27

Tasty Syllables

There are 15 three-syllable words related to foods mixed up in this puzzle. The beginning syllable is in Column A; the second syllable is in Column B; the third is in Column C. Each syllable will be used only once, so you can cross each one out as you use it.

	A	B	C
1.	B E V	A P	T I
2.	H A M	C O	R Y
3.	P O	G H E T	N A I S E
4.	C U	N I L	E R
5.	P I N E	B E	L A T E
6.	B R O C	B U R G	R O L E
7.	S P A	O N	A G E
8.	C H O C	C U M	E S
9.	S A N D	S E	T O
10.	V A	E R	C U E
11.	M A Y	W I C H	L A
12.	B A R	T A	B E R
13.	C A S	O	L A D E
14.	M A R	B E R	P L E
15.	S T R A W	M A	L I

1. _____
2. _____
3. _____
4. _____
5. _____
6. _____
7. _____
8. _____
9. _____
10. _____
11. _____
12. _____
13. _____
14. _____
15. _____

28

SYLLABLES

There are 14 three-syllable words mixed up in this puzzle. The beginning syllable is in Column A; the second syllable is in Column B; the third is in Column C. Each syllable is used only once, so you can cross each one out as you use it. The first word is ANYONE.

	A	B	C
1.	A N	D U C T	B A L L
2.	V A	G A	N O O N
3.	E X	Y	A D E
4.	B A S	A	T I O N
5.	A F	E	T E E N
6.	C R E	V I D	O N E
7.	M I	C A	R O W
8.	L E M	E N	R O O
9.	C O N	T E R	C I S E
10.	D I	M O R	T I V E
11.	T E L	O N	E D
12.	K A N	E R	S C O P E
13.	T O	K E T	O R
14.	S E V	C R O	P H O N E

1. _anyone_
2. _____
3. _____
4. _____
5. _____
6. _____
7. _____
8. _____
9. _____
10. _____
11. _____
12. _____
13. _____
14. _____

29

Syllable Match-up

The object of this word game is to combine all the syllables below into the words defined. You will use all the syllables, but only once. The blanks after the definitions tell you the number of letters in the word.

A   AL   AR   BAK   BE   BLE   BOT   CA   CAB   CAN   CIDE
CIR   CLE   CRET   DAN   DE   DY   ER   FAR   FER   GER   GIN
IN   JOUR   LOW   MOR   NEL   NEY   OF   PLE   PRE   RIVE   ROW
SIM   SE   TEND   THER   TION   TO   TOM   TUN   VA   Y

1. A round shape   __ __ __ __ __ __
2. Peril, risk   __ __ __ __ __ __
3. Easy, not completed   __ __ __ __ __ __ __
4. A bread and pastry shop   __ __ __ __ __
5. A holiday   __ __ __ __ __ __
6. To start   __ __ __ __
7. The day after today   __ __ __ __ __ __ __
8. Hidden   __ __ __ __ __ __
9. A sweet food with lots of sugar   __ __ __ __
10. A trip   __ __ __ __ __ __ __
11. To let   __ __ __ __ __
12. A small house   __ __ __ __ __ __
13. A passage cut through a hill   __ __ __ __ __ __ __
14. To make believe   __ __ __ __ __ __
15. The deepest part of anything   __ __ __ __ __ __ __
16. To settle   __ __ __ __ __ __
17. To volunteer   __ __ __ __ __
18. Capable   __ __ __ __
19. To come, appear   __ __ __ __ __ __
20. More distant   __ __ __ __ __ __

30

Prefixes

A *prefix* is a letter or group of letters that is put in front of a word to change the meaning of the word. See how many words you can make by using these prefixes.

pre-	un-	re-
preview	uncertain	repaint
pre	un	re
pre	un	re
pre	un	re
pre	un	re
pre	un	re
pre	un	re
pre	un	re
pre	un	re

de-	inter-	trans-
deform	interwoven	transport
de	inter	trans
de	inter	trans
de	inter	trans
de	inter	trans
de	inter	trans
de	inter	trans
de	inter	trans
de	inter	trans

A *suffix* is a letter or group of letters that is put at the end of a word to change the meaning of the word. See how many words you can make by adding these suffixes to words you know.

-ful	-ly	-ness
thankful	warmly	kindness
ful	ly	ness
ful	ly	ness
ful	ly	ness
ful	ly	ness
ful	ly	ness
ful	ly	ness
ful	ly	ness
ful	ly	ness
ful	ly	ness

-less	-er	-able
ageless	singer	workable
less	er	able
less	er	able
less	er	able
less	er	able
less	er	able
less	er	able
less	er	able
less	er	able

Compound words are made up of two smaller words. How many compounds can you make by combining the single words below in different ways? Thirty is a great score.

cast	wash	bed	butter	sales	play
home	cup	lock	eye	boat	work
rail	down	ply	ball	sun	touch
wood	sail	road	smith	lime	police
light	fly	foot	base	black	ground
rain	board	brow	man	mail	bow
lash	town	over	card	back	stone

1. _____
2. _____
3. _____
4. _____
5. _____
6. _____
7. _____
8. _____
9. _____
10. _____
11. _____
12. _____
13. _____
14. _____
15. _____
16. _____
17. _____
18. _____
19. _____
20. _____
21. _____
22. _____
23. _____
24. _____
25. _____
26. _____
27. _____
28. _____
29. _____
30. _____
31. _____
32. _____
33. _____
34. _____
35. _____
36. _____
37. _____
38. _____
39. _____
40. _____
41. _____
42. _____

There are three blanks in each of these sentences. In the first blank, write one of the compound words at the bottom of the page. The first half of the compound fits in the second blank; the last part fits in the third blank. The sentences must make sense.

1.   Carrying his _____, the lawyer entered the courtroom for a _____ session before his next _____.

2.   He thought the case was _____, but he went out for some fresh _____ to relieve a _____ feeling in his chest.

3.   The morning _____ prints all the latest _____ on thousands of pounds of _____.

4.   The teacher was already in the _____ when the _____ entered the _____.

5.   "Your studying should be done _____," she warned _____ she began to _____ out the assignment.

6.   Because of the amount of _____, the students were going _____ early to start their _____.

7.   He sat at the _____ wondering how many papers he would have to _____ before he was a good _____.

8.   The plants in the _____ were a different shade of _____ than those living in the _____.

9.   As the _____ warmed everything up, the plants turned toward the _____ so it would _____ directly on them.

10.   "_____ can learn to swim," said the instructor, as he turned to see if _____ of his students had his/her _____ wet.

CLASSROOM   BEFOREHAND   SUNSHINE   AIRTIGHT   TYPEWRITER
BRIEFCASE   GREENHOUSE   ANYBODY   NEWSPAPER   HOMEWORK

34

SPLIT COMPOUNDS

One of the compounds below fits in each sentence – the whole compound in the first blank, the first half in the second blank, and the last part in the third blank. Finish these sentences so they make sense.

TIGHTROPE   EVERYWHERE   HEAVYWEIGHT

1. Sally's dog loves to go _____ with her, and _____ afternoon he knows _____ to find her.

2. Learning to walk a _____ is easier if your muscles aren't _____ before you walk the _____.

3. The _____ boxer was too _____, so he had to lose _____.

Choose three of the compounds below to write split compound sentences like those above.

FOOTBALL   GREYHOUND   RAILROAD   SOMETIME   HEARTBEAT

1. _____
    _____

2. _____
    _____

3. _____
    _____

Think up some compound words and create some split compound sentences of your own here.

_____
_____
_____
_____
_____
_____

Word Building

Below are some three-letter words. You can make words of five or more letters from them by adding at least one letter to both the beginning and the end of each word. You may not use the letter S to end the word.

1. _____ ADE _____
2. _____ HIM _____
3. _____ ROT _____
4. _____ WAR _____
5. _____ RAW _____
6. _____ HUT _____
7. _____ OAR _____
8. _____ RUN _____

9. _____ ARC _____
10. _____ LID _____
11. _____ RAT _____
12. _____ PAR _____
13. _____ ROW _____
14. _____ HAS _____
15. _____ RAP _____
16. _____ OUR _____

You can make five-letter words out of the three-letter words listed below. Add two letters to the beginning of each word to make a new word. How many can you do?

1. _____ _____ INK
2. _____ _____ END
3. _____ _____ ILL
4. _____ _____ HER
5. _____ _____ BIN
6. _____ _____ ANT
7. _____ _____ EEL
8. _____ _____ ACE

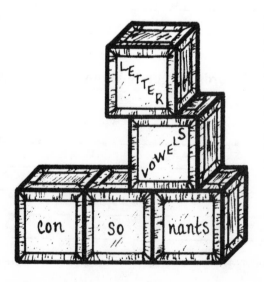

9. _____ _____ ORE
10. _____ _____ BIT
11. _____ _____ OWN
12. _____ _____ LAY
13. _____ _____ OIL
14. _____ _____ STY
15. _____ _____ DAM
16. _____ _____ LOW

36

Words rhyme when they sound alike at the end. Practice rhyming words by repeating the ending sounds of the words below. Use the back of the paper if you need more room.

rain	ball	tale	drop
rein		trail	
train			

Share your lists with classmates to see who had the most two and three-syllable words.

Rhyme Time

How many words can you think of that have the same ending sounds as the words below? Use the back of the paper if you need more room. When you are finished, compare your lists with classmates to see who had the most rhyming words and the most original.

nest	*true*	*clap*	*fan*
vest	crew		
dressed			

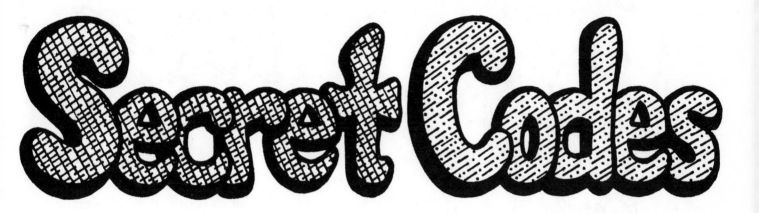

Codes are a fun way to send messages and spark curiosity in bulletin boards and interest centers. Decoding requires careful attention to spelling, and it involves our minds in that wonderful process by which we make intuitive leaps to solve problems. The word activities in this chapter explain codes and provide practice in deciphering codes.

Once your students work these pages, they may want to develop their own pages for the class to work. Students can write coded letters to parents or grandparents (including the key, of course); write notes to pen pals and secret pals; adopt a class code and have a message or assignment each day written on the chalkboard in that code; or make up tall tales to explain the origin of their codes, where they are/were used, by whom, when they were invented, etc.

SECRET CODES

Codes are a way to hide words from everyone but the sender and receiver of a secret message. A simple code substitutes one symbol (a letter or a word) for each letter in the original message. A coded message is called a *cipher*. Translating a secret message back to plain language with a key is called *deciphering*.

Remember - for a code to work, both the sender and the receiver must have a key to the code! Here's the key to a simple secret code which substitutes one letter for another in reverse alphabetical order.

ALPHABET: A B C D E F G H I J K L M N O P Q R S T U V W X Y Z
CODE: Z Y X W V U T S R Q P O N M L K J I H G F E D C B A

Use the key to decipher the secret message below! (Don't write on the line until you decipher the whole message.)
(DIRGV BLFI MZNV LM GSV ORMV YVOLD)

R _____ZN Z NZTMRURXVMG SFNZM YVRMT!!

Here's another simple secret code which substitutes a number for each letter in order.
ALPHABET:

A	B	C	D	E	F	G	H	I	J	K	L	M	N	O	P	Q	R	S	T	U	V	W	X	Y	Z
CODE: 1	2	3	4	5	6	7	8	9	10	11	12	13	14	15	16	17	18	19	20	21	22	23	24	25	26

Write a secret message using this code. Trade papers with a friend and decipher the messages.

CRYPTOGRAPHY

CRYPTOGRAPHY is the study of secret codes. A specialist in secret codes is called a **CRYPTOGRAPHER**. Here is a secret code that uses symbols other than letters and numbers.

A	B	C
D	E	F
G	H	I

J.	K.	L.
M.	N.	O.
P.	Q.	R.

CLUE: In this code you use only the lines and dots around the letters. Therefore an A is ⌐; a K is ⊔; an S is V; or a W is V.

O.K., CRYPTOGRAPHERS, use the key to decipher this secret message!

CRYPTO-GRAM

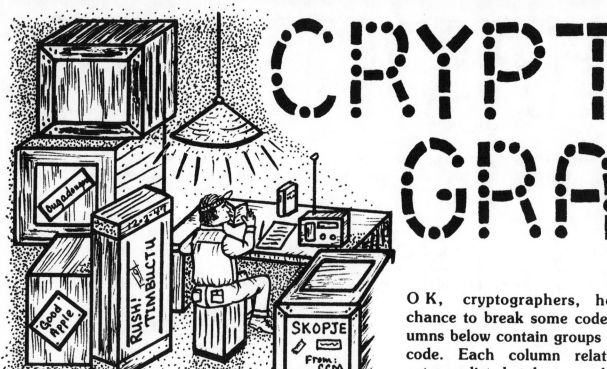

O K, cryptographers, here's your chance to break some codes. The columns below contain groups of words in code. Each column relates to the category listed at the top and has its own code. All three codes substitute a different set of letters for the letters in the alphabet. You must use the letters you know from the samples to help you decipher the other words in the group. Each word you figure out will give you more of the code. Good Luck!

CIRCUS ANIMALS

1. $\overset{\text{e l e p h a n t}}{\overline{X}\ \overline{R}\ \overline{X}\ \overline{G}\ \overline{K}\ \overline{J}\ \overline{Z}\ \overline{H}}$

2. $\overline{T}\ \overline{B}\ \overline{C}$

3. $\overline{K}\ \overline{B}\ \overline{W}\ \overline{D}\ \overline{X}$

4. $\overline{G}\ \overline{B}\ \overline{Z}\ \overline{P}$

5. $\overline{D}\ \overline{X}\ \overline{J}\ \overline{R}$

6. $\overline{C}\ \overline{B}\ \overline{W}\ \overline{N}\ \overline{R}\ \overline{R}\ \overline{J}$

7. $\overline{R}\ \overline{N}\ \overline{B}\ \overline{Z}$

8. $\overline{H}\ \overline{N}\ \overline{C}\ \overline{X}\ \overline{W}$

9. $\overline{Q}\ \overline{J}\ \overline{V}\ \overline{X}\ \overline{R}$

10. $\overline{R}\ \overline{X}\ \overline{B}\ \overline{G}\ \overline{J}\ \overline{W}\ \overline{T}$

THE PET SHOP

1. $\overset{\text{f l e a\quad p o w d e r}}{\overline{B}\ \overline{Y}\ \overline{A}\ \overline{C}\ \ \overline{I}\ \overline{W}\ \overline{G}\ \overline{S}\ \overline{A}\ \overline{H}}$

2. $\overline{M}\ \overline{C}\ \overline{N}\ \overline{A}$

3. $\overline{N}\ \overline{W}\ \overline{Y}\ \overline{S}\ \overline{B}\ \overline{T}\ \overline{U}\ \overline{O}$

4. $\overline{I}\ \overline{R}\ \overline{I}\ \overline{I}\ \overline{F}$

5. $\overline{I}\ \overline{A}\ \overline{Q}\ \ \overline{B}\ \overline{W}\ \overline{W}\ \overline{S}$

6. $\overline{D}\ \overline{T}\ \overline{H}\ \overline{S}\ \ \overline{U}\ \overline{A}\ \overline{A}\ \overline{S}$

7. $\overline{Z}\ \overline{T}\ \overline{Q}\ \overline{Q}\ \overline{A}\ \overline{P}$

8. $\overline{Q}\ \overline{R}\ \overline{H}\ \overline{Q}\ \overline{Y}\ \overline{A}$

9. $\overline{O}\ \overline{C}\ \overline{J}\ \overline{U}\ \overline{Q}\ \overline{A}\ \overline{H}$

10. $\overline{M}\ \overline{C}\ \overline{P}\ \overline{C}\ \overline{H}\ \overline{F}$

THE SODA FOUNTAIN

1. $\overset{\text{m i l k\quad s h a k e}}{\overline{H}\ \overline{E}\ \overline{I}\ \overline{J}\ \ \overline{T}\ \overline{F}\ \overline{R}\ \overline{J}\ \overline{G}}$

2. $\overline{T}\ \overline{N}\ \overline{S}\ \overline{A}\ \overline{R}\ \overline{G}$

3. $\overline{E}\ \overline{B}\ \overline{G}\ \ \overline{B}\ \overline{U}\ \overline{G}\ \overline{R}\ \overline{H}$

4. $\overline{I}\ \overline{G}\ \overline{H}\ \overline{K}\ \overline{S}\ \overline{R}\ \overline{A}\ \overline{G}$

5. $\overline{H}\ \overline{R}\ \overline{I}\ \overline{V}$

6. $\overline{U}\ \overline{K}\ \overline{K}\ \overline{V}\ \ \overline{M}\ \overline{G}\ \overline{G}\ \overline{U}$

7. $\overline{M}\ \overline{R}\ \overline{S}\ \overline{R}\ \overline{S}\ \overline{R}\ \ \overline{T}\ \overline{Z}\ \overline{I}\ \overline{E}\ \overline{V}$

8. $\overline{F}\ \overline{K}\ \overline{V}\ \ \overline{B}\ \overline{F}\ \overline{K}\ \overline{B}\ \overline{K}\ \overline{I}\ \overline{R}\ \overline{V}\ \overline{G}$

9. $\overline{T}\ \overline{F}\ \overline{G}\ \overline{U}\ \overline{M}\ \overline{G}\ \overline{V}$

10. $\overline{Z}\ \overline{N}\ \overline{A}\ \overline{A}\ \overline{E}\ \overline{S}\ \overline{C}$

Write Your Own Code

Use letters, numbers, symbols or whatever you would like to create your own code. Share the code with a friend, then send a message.

MY VERY OWN CODE

A	B	C	D	E	F	G	H	I	J	K	L	M

N	O	P	Q	R	S	T	U	V	W	X	Y	Z

SAFE T. FIRST

SAFE CO.

#1 Codes to Crack

Here are some cryptograms grouped into "crypto-families." Each word in a column is related to the same topic, and each column has a separate code. The sample will help you decode the other words in the family.

SPORTS	FOOD	HOLIDAYS

SPORTS

l a c r o s s e
R X M B J F F Q

F J M M Q B

W J J G P X R R

P X F Q P X R R

V J M T Q Y

G B X M T

B J R R Q B   F T X G Z S D

G Q S S Z F

D Y A S X F G Z M F

P X F T Q G P X R R

Z M Q   F T X G Z S D

C J D D Z S D

O J R R Q Y P X R R

P X H A Z S G J S

FOOD

r o a s t   b e e f
F A Z I Q   C X X N

I K Z O S X Q Q V

S Z T C G F O X F

T Z W L M V D S X I

Q G W Z   D Z I I X F A J X

N F V X L   D S V D Y X W

T Z D Z F A W V

K A Q Z Q A   I Z J Z L

K Z W D Z Y X I

I Q X Z Y

D S A M   T X V W

K A F Y   D S A K I

Q G F Y X R

N F X W D S   N F V X I

HOLIDAYS

V a l e n t i n e's   D a y
C G F T S W M S T'B   Q G E

O Y V M B W Z G B

Y G S R A A G Y

Y G F F H K T T S

W Y G S A B X M C M S X

F G J H V   Q G E

T G B W T V

Z H W Y T V'B   Q G E

L H R V W Y   H L   U R F E

O H F R Z J R B   Q G E

L G W Y T V'B   Q G E

Z T Z H V M G F   Q G E

C T W T V G S B   Q G E

S T K   E T G V'B   Q G E

44

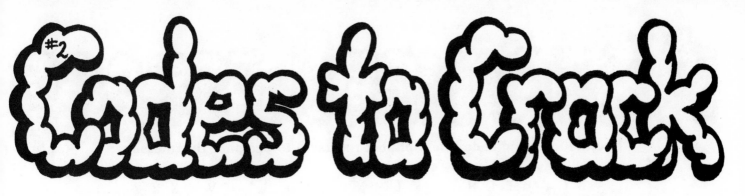

Each of these "crypto-families" has a different code. Can you decipher all the words in each column?

SCHOOL	FLOWERS	ORCHESTRA INSTRUMENTS
s o c i a l s t u d i e s	s n a p d r a g o n	c l a r i n e t
D T Q Z K X D O V U Z L D	N Y D T J O D P U Y	O Z C S U B F N
O L K Q P L J	Q U Y K B N T F W X K	N S W V E F N
D O V U L R O	J D R N B	J U R Z U B
X L K J R Z R Y Q L R O L J	T K M T Y R D	R M R F
D G L X X Z R Y	E I M M K O F I T	Q Z W N F
K J Z O P E L O Z Q	N M U F W	N S R V M R B F
J L K U Z R Y	J D L L U J R X	M C L L R R B
P T E L W T J I	A R Y Y R D	Y C S E
G J Z R Q Z G K X	T D Y N B	E U C B R
S J Z O Z R Y	H R U X K M	J U R Z C
Q X K D D J T T E	R O R N	Q S F B O Y Y R S B
D Q Z L R Q L	P K O D Y R I Z	O F Z Z R
X Z F J K J C	O U N K	A F N N Z F I S W V
D O V U C	T U T T B	M C L L

45

A STRANGE MESSAGE

Use the following code (the alphabet reversed) to decipher this message:

A B C D E F G H I J K L M N O P Q R S T U V W X Y Z
Z Y X W V U T S R Q P O N M L K J I H G F E D C B A

7 WIZXL 5097

UVOOLD XLOLMRHGH,

GSV NLGSVI HSRK UILN ALIVC OZMWVW LM VZIGS OZHG DVVP (VZIGS GRNV) RM KVIF. LFI LMVMVHH ERHRGVW GSV BFXZGZM ZMW VTBKG YVULIV NLERMT GSV HSRK GL RGH KIVHVMG OLXZGRLM. RG MLD ZDZRGH LFI TZGSVIRMT. XOLHV BLFI VBVH ZMW YIVZGSV WVVKOB. OVG LFI NRMWH IVEVZO GSV HSRK'H OLXZGRLM. LFI LMVMVHH DROO WRIVXG LFI DZB. UVZI ML SFNZM RMGVIEVMGRLM; GSV HSRK RH Z URUGS WRNVMHRLMZO NLWVO, RMERHRYOV GL MLINZO VZIGS VBVH. DV NZB ZGGVMW GSV TZGSVIRMT LU NRMWH RM LFI VZIGS ULINH LI GSILFTS ZHGIZO KILQVXGRLM. GSLHV FHRMT MLMSFNZM ULINH, LI ZHHRTMVW GL FMWVIDZGVI OREVH DROO FHV ZHGIZO KLDVIH.

KVZXV, LMV-LU-FH

Stretch your mental muscles, enjoy yourself, and have a good laugh! All of these are very healthy things to do, and all of them are involved in this chapter's activities. Practice looking at things more flexibly. Open your mind to new sources of ideas and that exciting intuitive process. These word games use parts of our minds we often ignore. Beware! These activities are fun, intriguing, and they may wake you up in the night with just ONE more!

These puzzles represent expressions we use. Solve them by carefully noticing the positions of the words and pictures. Are they under, over, mixed-up, inside, or a certain size?

stand I _I understand_	man board _____	cover agent _____	wear long _____
EZ iiii _____	$\dfrac{i}{8}$ _____	his iii O O O _____	G O I N G A R O U N D _____
CHAIR _____	TIRE _____	T O W N _____	ROADS (scattered) _____
b sick ed _____	DKI _____	G R U the block N I N N _____	EGSG GESG SEGG SGEG _____

More Position Puzzles...

he § art	ar up ms	every|right|thing	LO $\frac{HEAD}{HEELS}$ VE
$\frac{KNEE}{LIGHTS}$	R/E/A/D/I/N/G	ter very esting	FRIENDS $\frac{standing}{miss}$ FRIENDS
F I G H T	WALKING	time time	TOUCH
ground feet feet feet feet feet feet	one kind another one kind another one kind another one kind another one kind another one kind another	TAKE ONE MEAL TAKE ONE MEAL TAKE ONE MEAL	DICE DICE
C O S T S	1,000, **1**,000	I S O C K	$\frac{O}{M.D.}$ B.A. Ph.D.

My Very Own Puzzles

By _____

Make up some puzzles of your own and let a friend solve them!

Quit following me: _____	_____	looking over my shoulder	_____
_____	 _____	_____	_____
_____	_____	_____	_____
_____	_____	 _____	_____

50

PUN-CTURES

A PUN is a play on words, or the humorous use of the word. A PUN-CTURE is a picture pun. Here are some pictures which show other meanings of common words. Fill in the pictures and create your own pun-ctures in the boxes below.

SPRING CLEANING	ICYCLE	SKI RESORT	
WALL HANGING	LOG JAM	TURKEY DRESSING	CUPCAKE
BUTTERFLY	MAILBOX	CAR POOL	HOT DOG

Sports Pun-ctures

A PUN is a play on words, or the humorous use of a word. A PUN-CTURE is a picture pun. Below are some sports pictures which show other meanings of common words. Fill in the remaining boxes with your own pun-ctures.

SPRING TRAINING

A HOME RUN

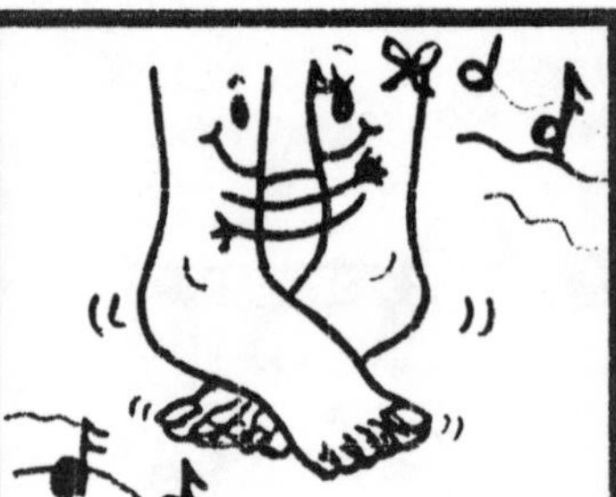

FOOTBALL

WATER SKIING

BOXING

DRAG RACING

TRAMPOLINE

SCUBA DIVING

Vocabulary games challenge us to recognize words we are familiar with in a new setting and require us to search our minds for seldom used words. Calling both to mind enriches our lives and our ability to express ourselves. This chapter provides some activities for increasing vocabulary, practicing alphabet skills, categorizing, plus a list of 180 words which could be used for daily learning, and a team game which stimulates interest in the dictionary and flexibility with word meanings.

Word Oval

There are thirty-eight words hidden in the oval below. Follow the arrows clockwise without skipping any letters, and see how many you can find. For example, starting with S on the left, you can find SURF and FACE. Words must have two or more letters. 28 = Good, 33 = Very Good, 37 = Excellent

The oval reads: SURFACENTERRACEASTEREAL MOSYEARTHUMPAIRPLANETOS

1. _____

2. _____   11. _____   20. _____   29. _____

3. _____   12. _____   21. _____   30. _____

4. _____   13. _____   22. _____   31. _____

5. _____   14. _____   23. _____   32. _____

6. _____   15. _____   24. _____   33. _____

7. _____   16. _____   25. _____   34. _____

8. _____   17. _____   26. _____   35. _____

9. _____   18. _____   27. _____   36. _____

10. _____   19. _____   28. _____   37. _____

                                                                   38. _____

The object of this word game is to write sentences using the letters in the words below. You will use each letter to start one word in your sentence. Here's an example with the word SPIRIT: *Some People Imagine Really Interesting Tales.* The beginning letters from each word in the sentence spell out the original word. Use your imagination!

relax _____

learn _____

enjoy _____

know _____

believe _____

give _____

love _____

peace _____

serve _____

friend _____

truth _____

power _____

beauty _____

better _____

calm _____

happy _____

rich _____

contentment _____

_____

Make word pyramids with the letters listed below. Add one letter at a time to make new words, and write them underneath in the shape of a pyramid. You may rearrange the letters. See how long you can make your pyramids. Use another sheet of paper if you need more room.

R   A   A   T

OR
FOR
FORE
FORGE
FORGET
FORGETS

M   S   N   R

O   E

For a greater challenge, don't change the order of the letters. You can also reverse the pattern by starting with a long word and _dropping_ a letter each time. For example, ASHTRAYS is a good word with which to start.

ALPHABET SOUP

Insert a different letter of the alphabet into each of the twenty-six empty boxes to complete a word of five or more letters reading across. The missing letter you add may be from any place in the word. You will use each letter of the alphabet only once, so cross each one off as you use it. All the letters on each line are not part of the hidden word.

A B C D E F G H I J K L M N O P Q R S T U V W X Y Z

O	M	T	G	I	**G**	A	N	T	I	C	M
E	R	B	I	C		C	L	E	T	G	S
M	Z	A	Y	E		T	R	A	X	L	E
U	I	P	U	P		E	T	S	G	N	F
S	C	K	I	C		B	A	L	L	D	L
T	F	S	C	H		O	L	H	Z	M	I
L	P	E	N	C		L	G	U	J	O	K
I	H	O	M	E		O	R	K	B	D	S
E	Q	T	J	C		A	Y	O	N	S	H
T	E	A	C	H		R	D	N	P	R	S
B	N	F	U	Z		Y	G	T	L	N	M
C	R	B	U	B		L	E	S	Q	Z	E
Q	A	N	I	M		L	V	B	L	T	Q
Z	X	Y	T	E		E	P	H	O	N	E
N	I	G	H	T		A	R	E	X	O	T
I	Y	Z	R	E		U	E	S	T	K	H
C	Q	R	X	E		E	R	Y	D	A	Y
O	G	S	K	I		U	M	P	J	U	L
Z	E	L	E	P		A	N	T	V	I	K
O	C	I	R	C		S	W	L	H	F	E
M	C	H	E	E		A	H	G	I	X	R
Z	F	I	R	E		L	Y	D	R	Q	A
T	Y	C	R	I		K	E	T	S	F	I
F	A	N	T	A		T	I	C	V	L	E
P	L	A	Y	I		G	R	T	N	H	K
R	G	C	A	N		Y	W	C	E	Q	N

TRY IT TODAY!

Soooo good for you!

Yummy!

57

ALPHABET SOUP

Insert a different letter of the alphabet into each of the twenty-six empty boxes to complete a word of five or more letters reading across. The letter you add may be in any place in the word. You will use each letter of the alphabet only once, so cross each one off as you use it. All the letters on each line are not part of the hidden word.

A B C D E F G H I J K L M N O P Q R S T U V W X Y Z

A	M	C	E	L	E	**P**	H	A	N	T	C	E
C	L	A	B	E	A		T	Y	E	M	O	N
E	F	O	R	G	I		E	L	Y	S	N	O
V	S	E	H	A	R		O	N	Y	E	V	T
D	A	S	W	U	N		V	E	R	S	E	Z
E	M	W	H	O	L		N	E	S	S	I	P
T	I	G	H	E	A		T	H	Y	A	M	O
M	O	Y	A	B	U		D	A	N	C	E	Q
P	R	M	P	R	O		P	E	R	I	T	Y
L	A	R	A	I	N		O	W	D	E	R	K
O	B	X	T	E	N		O	Y	M	E	N	T
F	I	S	P	A	R		L	E	R	G	I	E
T	J	P	O	X	A		R	E	E	S	L	E
S	A	C	H	E	E		F	U	L	Z	O	N
Y	C	O	N	F	I		E	N	C	E	T	E
E	V	W	A	M	A		I	N	G	F	A	L
T	O	H	A	P	P		G	L	M	O	N	T
I	E	Z	G	R	E		T	E	R	M	L	S
S	D	E	L	I	G		T	F	U	L	N	G
A	C	R	E	L	A		A	T	I	O	N	B
I	F	G	P	E	A		E	K	E	L	O	N
K	Z	R	E	N	E		X	O	V	A	N	T
M	O	R	S	D	P		S	I	T	I	V	E
S	E	N	P	E	R		E	C	T	L	T	E
M	O	E	X	C	I		E	M	E	N	T	L
S	A	G	L	N	Z		U	I	E	T	L	Y

DELICIOUS!

NEW

TRY IT!

Antonyms are words with opposite meanings. There are twenty-eight words below whose opposites are listed at the bottom of the page. Choose an antonym for each word and write it on the line.

1. early _____
2. find _____
3. half _____
4. give _____
5. inside _____
6. bottom _____
7. loss _____
8. open _____
9. hate _____
10. forget _____
11. ugly _____
12. happy _____
13. work _____
14. sharp _____

15. joy _____
16. adult _____
17. broad _____
18. join _____
19. hazy _____
20. strange _____
21. negative _____
22. question _____
23. public _____
24. poor _____
25. mend _____
26. warm _____
27. danger _____
28. noisy _____

sad	safety	love		
shut	cool	remember	damage	sorrow
child	lose	separate	play	quiet
narrow	whole	positive	wealthy	pretty
top	reply	outside	dull	receive
late	gain	familiar	private	clear

SYNONYM GAME

A synonym is a word which means the same or nearly the same as another word. Below are fourteen words with three blanks beside each one. Choose three synonyms for each word from the list at the bottom of the page, and write them in the blanks. For example, a synonym of MONEY is FUNDS.

1. MONEY _____ _____ _____
2. SILENT _____ _____ _____
3. CHANGE _____ _____ _____
4. ANTICIPATE _____ _____ _____
5. SURE _____ _____ _____
6. SMALL _____ _____ _____
7. STRENGTH _____ _____ _____
8. INTELLIGENT _____ _____ _____
9. QUESTION _____ _____ _____
10. LARGE _____ _____ _____
11. POSSIBLE _____ _____ _____
12. LOUD _____ _____ _____
13. QUICK _____ _____ _____
14. PREDICT _____ _____ _____

VARY	FORETELL	VIGOR	NOISY	QUIET	DIMINUTIVE
CERTAIN	BRIGHT	WEALTH	ENORMOUS	ALTER	UPROARIOUS
PROMPT	SHIFT	EXPECT	SEARCH	FORECAST	UNMISTAKABLE
LITTLE	VITALITY	BOOMING	LIKELY	CASH	QUICK-WITTED
VAST	HOPE FOR	STILL	LIMITED	SEEK	CREDIBLE
SWIFT	PROPHESY	FAST	FORCE	IMMENSE	SOUNDLESS
FUNDS	AWAIT	KEEN	POSITIVE	INQUIRE	ACHIEVABLE

Colorful Synonyms

Below are groups of four words related to colors. On the line beside each group, write the correct synonym from the list at the right. You may also want to substitute some of these words for the common color words in your future creative writing.

1. scarlet, vermilion, crimson, cherry _____   orange

2. sapphire, azure, navy, indigo_____   purple

3. pale, sallow, dull, pallid _____   different colors

4. lemon, amber, flaxen, sunny _____   gray

5. tawny, mahogany, tan, chocolate_____   red

6. hue, tone, shade, dye _____   colorless

7. snowy, milky, frosty, ivory _____   black

8. plum, lavender, lilac, violet _____   color

9. rich, vivid, deep, intense_____   blue

10. pitch, ink, soot, ebony_____   yellow

11. verdant, emerald, olive, kelly_____   bright colors

12. dun, ashen, silver, leaden _____   white

13. plaid, checked, striped, variegated _____   brown

14. apricot, gold, brass, peach_____   green

HOMONYMS

Homonyms are words which sound alike but have different meanings. See if you can think up a homonym for each of the words below. Numbers 33-40 have more than one homonym. Give yourself 1 point for each homonym you get; then add 1 point for correct spelling.

75 points = Good, 80 points = Very Good, and 90 or more = Excellent

1. PLANE _____
2. MADE _____
3. HERE _____
4. PAIN _____
5. HALL _____
6. HEARD _____
7. BALL _____
8. SIZE _____
9. WAY _____
10. PALE _____
11. HORSE _____
12. STEAK _____
13. MAIL _____
14. BORED _____
15. NIGHT _____
16. ALOUD _____
17. CELLAR _____
18. THREW _____
19. WOULD _____
20. SALE _____

21. ATE _____
22. PAST _____
23. STEAL _____
24. HOLE _____
25. OUR _____
26. GREAT _____
27. MAIN _____
28. PATIENTS _____
29. FOUL _____
30. MOWN _____
31. CHOOSE _____
32. CEREAL _____
33. RAIN _____
34. ROAD _____
35. SOW _____
36. CITE _____
37. THEIR _____
38. CENTS _____
39. PRAYS _____
40. RIGHT _____

62

Categorizing

Figure out which twelve words belong in each category and write them on the lines.

green pepper	gardenia	nectarine	cabbage	daisy
carrot	carnation	cucumber	grapefruit	peach
daffodil	turnip	orange	spinach	broccoli
cantaloupe	tangerine	poinsettia	tulip	watermelon
marigold	asparagus	apricot	petunia	Brussels sprouts
corn	guava	chrysanthemum	mango	geranium
violet	celery	banana	orchid	cauliflower
pineapple				

Fruits   Vegetables   Flowers

_____   _____   _____

_____   _____   _____

_____   _____   _____

_____   _____   _____

_____   _____   _____

_____   _____   _____

_____   _____   _____

_____   _____   _____

People, Places & Things

See if you can put each of these forty-eight words into the correct category.

contractor	instruments	school	pilot	telescope	airport
license	clinic	mechanic	actor	textbook	observatory
theater	artifact	professor	airplane	architect	auditorium
archeologist	machinery	county	reporter	university	consultation
computer	laboratory	astronomer	horse	counselor	data processor
microscope	jockey	garden	contract	classroom	newspaper
factory	lecture	student	office	electrician	investment
engineer	landscaper	racetrack	courtroom	equipment	museum

PEOPLE   PLACES   THINGS

_____   _____   _____

_____   _____   _____

_____   _____   _____

_____   _____   _____

_____   _____   _____

_____   _____   _____

_____   _____   _____

_____   _____   _____

_____   _____   _____

_____   _____   _____

_____   _____   _____

PARTS of SPEECH

Categorize each of the words below as a *NOUN* (the name of a person, place or thing), an *ADJECTIVE* (a word that describes a person, place, or thing), or a *VERB* (an action word).

friend	joyful	choose	eager	music
excellent	captain	beautiful	enjoy	delightful
free	happy	learn	curious	plant
beach	receive	celebrate	passenger	relax
listen	reptile	newsworthy	cheerful	sunset
creative	prefer	valuable	agree	soft
finish	draw	microscope	renew	photograph
peaceful	money	brave	governor	accept
mountain	laugh	planet	vibrate	zoo

NOUNS   ADJECTIVES   VERBS

NOUNS	ADJECTIVES	VERBS
1. _____	1. _____	1. _____
2. _____	2. _____	2. _____
3. _____	3. _____	3. _____
4. _____	4. _____	4. _____
5. _____	5. _____	5. _____
6. _____	6. _____	6. _____
7. _____	7. _____	7. _____
8. _____	8. _____	8. _____
9. _____	9. _____	9. _____
10. _____	10. _____	10. _____
11. _____	11. _____	11. _____
12. _____	12. _____	12. _____
13. _____	13. _____	13. _____
14. _____	14. _____	14. _____
15. _____	15. _____	15. _____

START

ENTRANCE

The object of this game is to see if you can fill in all the blank spaces below. Your words begin with the letter above the column and fit the category at the left. For example, a boy's name starting with T could be Thomas.

	T	H	I	N	K
BOYS' NAMES					
GIRLS' NAMES					
CITIES					
STATES					
COUNTRIES					

	D	R	E	A	M
PRESENTS					
FOOD					
TREES					
ANIMALS					
PLACES					

	S	T	A	R	T
TIME					
SPORTS					
VERBS					
CLOTHES					
PLANTS					

The object of this game is to fill in all the spaces below. Your words must begin with the letter above the column and fit the category at the left. For example, a holiday starting with M could be Memorial Day.

	M	A	T	C	H
HOLIDAYS					
CARS					
DRINKS					
TV SHOWS					
GAMES					

	G	R	O	W	S
COLORS					
NOUNS					
VERBS					
ADJECTIVES					
FRUITS					

	S	H	A	R	P
FLOWERS					
BIRDS					
SONGS					
WEATHER					
BUILDINGS					

These will challenge your concentration, vocabulary, and spelling. Fill in the charts below with the ending of one word starting the next. The second word must begin with the last letter of the first; the first letter of the third word must be the same as the final letter of the second word; and so on. Here are two examples.

TOOLS	wrencH	HammeR	RakE	Electric drill
FLOWERS	daffodiL	LilaC	CarnatioN	Nasturtium

ANIMALS				
SPORTS				
LANGUAGE				
INSECTS				

TREES				
VEHICLES				
FRUITS				
DANCES				
COLORS				

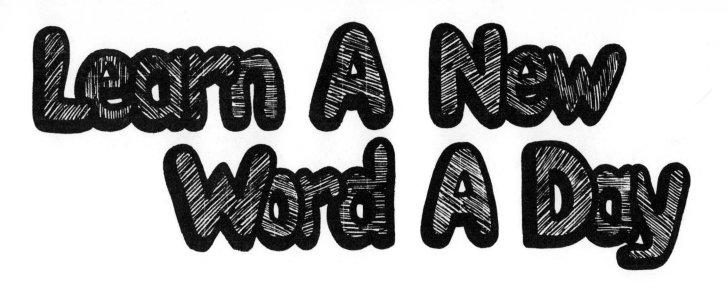

Learn A New Word A Day

Here is a list of 180 words that can be used as a year-long vocabulary list. The words are intended to be challenging and encourage students to look at familiar words more closely. Your word choices will depend on your own preferences and the level of your students. In view of research on vocabulary development, it's important to carefully choose the words we present to children. The difference between the vocabulary of a good reader and a poor reader at the kindergarten level is around 3,000 words. By the time these readers reach the fifth grade (some 900 school days later) that vocabulary difference has increased ten times! If we could successfully teach 20 new words each day of school, we would still not keep up. With this in mind, it seems appropriate to use wisdom and quality in our word selection. This word list comes from the more positive end of the spectrum in order to focus attention on what works best in life.

LEARN A NEW WORD A DAY - Suggested words for daily study

NOUNS		VERBS		ADJECTIVES	
enthusiasm	compassion	innovate	invigorate	original	magnetic
opportunity	inspiration	revitalize	stimulate	creative	unbiased
enlightenment	contribution	communicate	praise	courageous	candid
instinct	talent	acknowledge	celebrate	inventive	thoughtful
contentment	calmness	organize	protect	aggressive	rational
potential	intellect	design	integrate	decisive	realistic
cooperation	wisdom	empathize	balance	independent	visionary
diplomacy	personality	appreciate	clarify	dynamic	convergent
consideration	assurance	energize	manifest	magnificent	divergent
partnership	realization	reinforce	rejuvenate	adaptable	assertive
harmony	companionship	analyze	discern	gentle	experimental
peace	relationship	synthesize	ignite	patient	humorous
discipline	confidence	supervise	perform	sensitive	theoretical
persistence	serenity	counsel	encounter	versatile	inquisitive
power	gratitude	convince	contemplate	popular	vulnerable
optimism	aspiration	unify	activate	intense	literal
motivation	humility	recognize	applaud	practical	figurative
impression	tolerance	comprehend	congratulate	industrious	auspicious
expression	approval	illumine	motivate	loyal	provident
affection	friendship	renew	speculate	sincere	capable
imagination	emotion	prosper	educate	dependable	credible
fulfillment	knowledge	perceive	improvise	adventurous	effortless
endurance	understanding	support	consummate	curious	ingenious
dexterity	abundance	persevere	research	gracious	courteous
structure	spectrum	reward	transform	clever	
intuition	paradox	generate		sympathetic	
catalyst	tintinnabulation	enrich		resourceful	
challenge	onomatopoeia	accomplish		idealistic	
responsibility	premonition	meditate		conscientious	
experience	mastery	promote		generous	
conscious	preference	forgive		broadminded	
success	phenomenon	encourage		poised	
judgment				trustworthy	
				prudent	

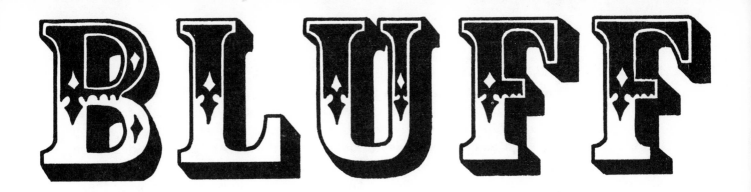

BLUFF is a word definition game which increases vocabulary, promotes flexible use of language, and exercises verbal and role-playing skills.

THE BASIC GAME

Bluff is a team game with a format similar to charades. A strange or difficult word is given to one of two teams to define. Each member of the defining team receives a slip of paper, supposedly having the word's definition on it. Only one slip has the word and its definition; the others say "BLUFF." Each member in turn gives a different definition for the word. The object is to fool the opponents, who must guess (as a group) which answer is correct. A point is scored by the successful team - the defining team if they bluff well enough, the guessing team if they figure out the correct definition.

PREPARATION

Before the game, someone looks up three to ten strange and interesting words in the dictionary and writes the definition of each on a slip of paper. Nouns and verbs are the easiest. The teacher will probably want to do the word selection at first. All slips of paper for the game should be the same size and opaque. Those slips without definitions should say "BLUFF."

SAMPLE DEFINITIONS

The more examples discussed before the game, the quicker the players will catch on and enjoy the game. Students will gradually become more familiar with dictionary format and phrase their definitions accordingly. Here are two sample definitions a player bluffing might think up.

"The _____ is a South American bird which lives in the tallest trees in the jungle. It is multicolored and eats large insects."
"The _____ is an artifact found in an African archeological dig."

HOW TO PLAY

The members of the starting team receive slips of paper, as the teacher (or moderator) announces the word. Members of the defining team carefully examine their papers, reading the definitions or making up their bluffs. It is important that no talking is done and that the slips of paper are concealed from everyone. If anyone knows the real word meaning, nothing should be said until the end of the round. If that person is bluffing, he/she should continue to do so; if the person is on the guessing team, he/she will enable the team to get the point.

As the members of the starting team take turns defining, the opponents carefully watch behavior, body language, ease of defining, and other clues to the correct answer or the person with it. The definers will soon learn to cover up clues given by their teammates, such as copying styles of defining. If the person with the definition reads it right off the paper in an obvious way, teammates can pretend to do the same thing and lead the guessers off the track. If the definers are clever, the opposing team will have a difficult time deciding.

When all definitions are given, the second team decides which answer was correct. A point goes to the successful team, and the next round begins with the second team defining.

WHY PLAY BLUFF?

BLUFF is a fun game which better acquaints students with dictionary format, especially as they begin looking up words for the game. BLUFF encourages flexible use of words, thinking quickly, speaking in front of others, plus observing nonverbal communication. A great deal of cleverness and imaginative thinking are involved in the game, and recall increases dramatically when anything is learned in a fun atmosphere.

SAMPLE WORDS

batman (băt´mən) n. a soldier in the British Army assigned to an officer as a servant

genipap (jĕn´ĭ păp´) n. a brown edible fruit, about the size of an orange, from a tropical American tree

ha-ha (hä´hä´) n. a barrier consisting of a trench or ditch; a sunken fence

ilex (ī´lĕks)n. 1) the evergreen oak, holm oak, 2) any tree or shrub in the holly family

keek (kēk) v. to peep or spy

lev (lĕf) n. a copper coin, the monetary unit of Bulgaria

sea hog (sē hog) n. a porpoise (Words that seem obvious can be fun, also.)

thaumatology (thô´mə tŏl´ə jē) n. the study of miracles

WHAT'S IN A NAME?

This chapter has activities dealing with our names and creating fun names for others. Because names are so important and personal, your students may want to find out more about their own names -- where each came from, who they were named after, what the names originally meant, and how to say theirs in a foreign language. Students can also make up names for imaginary streets, cities, states or countries, and place them on a map; think up fitting names of sports teams (ferocious, alliterative, silly or significant); and they can use their full names for a word mine game.

Some of us are happy with the names we have, some would like a different one, and others would change names from time to time. Deciding what name we would most like to have is an intriguing exercise. Have students choose perfect names, and think briefly about what they would most like to do in life (fantasy is very appropriate!). Then have them pretend they are at a party where they circulate, introduce themselves, and tell what they do or who they are. This is a fun way to experience a dream and get clear on whether or not it really fits.

MAKE YOUR VERY OWN NAME POSTER, ALL ABOUT YOU !!!

What are your preferences, your favorite people, places and things? Make a terrific poster for your room, your parents, your grandparents, Open House, or to share with your classmates!

Practice printing your name in big, FAT letters that fill up a whole page. When you are satisfied with your lettering, print your name on a large piece of butcher paper or poster board, for example; any size is fine, the bigger, the better. Fill in the letters with ideas, drawings, photographs, and other things that interest you personally. Give your poster added eye appeal by using crayons, markers, magazine pictures, colored chalk, and more. Have fun and enjoy yourself!

HERE ARE SOME POSSIBLE TOPICS TO SPARK YOUR IMAGINATION!

Friends	Things that make me happy	Sports	Sounds I like
Pets	Movies	I laugh when…	If I could BE…DO…HAVE anything
Favorite places	Songs	Books I've enjoyed	at all…
Foods I like	I'm good at…	Things I like to do	
TV shows		Colors	
		School subjects	
		Exciting moments	
		When I grow up…	

74

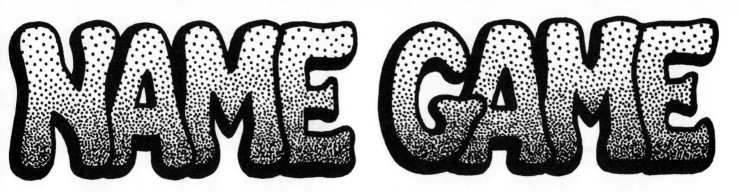

Read these funny names which form phrases, then use your imagination to "C. Hominy" you can think up yourself. Share your finished products with your friends for a good laugh.

Belle E. Laugh	Ed. G. Nerves	Otto Mobile
Ira Fuse	Sam Antics	C. Shell
Avery Goodman	Bud E. System	C. Garr
Beau Ring	Austin Tashious	Statia Nery
Jenn U. Wine	B.D. Eyes	B.A. Winner

Here are some initials to help you get started:

I. M	C. A.	U. R. (R. U.)	C. F.	G. I.
B.	U. B.	C. U. (U. C.)	I. C.	G. U.

You will come up with many more! Jesse F. U. Can....

_____

_____

_____

_____

_____

_____

_____

_____

_____

_____

_____

_____

_____

Books & Authors

These fanciful books were written by some fitting authors. Enjoy the humor and get involved!

A DOG'S LIFE	by	Ken L. Keeper
LOVING RELATIONSHIPS	by	Bea Friend
MY PLEDGE OF HONOR	by	Lowell T. Oath
HOW TO IMPROVE YOUR LOOKS	by	B. U. Tiffle
THERE'S NO ROOM AT THE TOP	by	S. R. Dean
CONFESSIONS OF A CRIMINAL	by	Jules Thief
WE BIT THE DUST	by	Al E. Mow
BEING OBJECTIVE	by	Ivan Openmind
FAMILY OF MAN	by	Olive N. Peace

NOW, YOU TOO CAN CREATE, O. Eugenious

_____ by Justin Case

_____ by B. A. Gardener

_____ by Seymour Clearly

_____ by Eliza Little

_____ by Claire Voyant

_____ by Ophelia Muscles

_____

_____

_____

_____

_____

WRITTEN BY _____

MORE Fun With Names

The names and book titles below relate to the movies, animals and occupations. Add more names and books to these categories, or make up some new ones on the lines.

THE MOVIES - *Success at Last,* by I. Minda Limelight

Otto B. Astar	Mel O. Drama	Polly Chrome
Dee Rector	Cory O'Graffer	Cary A. Torch
Claus D. Signer	Mae Cupp	M. U. Late

_____

_____

_____

_____

ANIMALS - *My Transformation*, by Matt A. Morphus, as told to Kate E. Pillar

Sally Mander	Al E. Gator	Annie Maul
Ty Gress	Ellie Phant	G. Raffe
Al Paca	Tadd Pole	Adolph Finn

_____

_____

_____

_____

OCCUPATIONS - *How to Lay Carpets*, by Walter Wall

Mort Ishan	Phillip R. Tank	P. D. O'Trician
Phil Ossifer	E. Lectrician	Minnie Stir
Sy Cologist	Ray D. Ologist	Otto McKanic

_____

_____

_____

_____

George Washington

Our famous first President, George Washington, had many letters in his name. Use these letters as many times as they occur in his name, and see how many different words you can make. 50 words = Fine, 70 = Very Good, 85 = Terrific, 100 = Excellent! You may need a second sheet of paper.

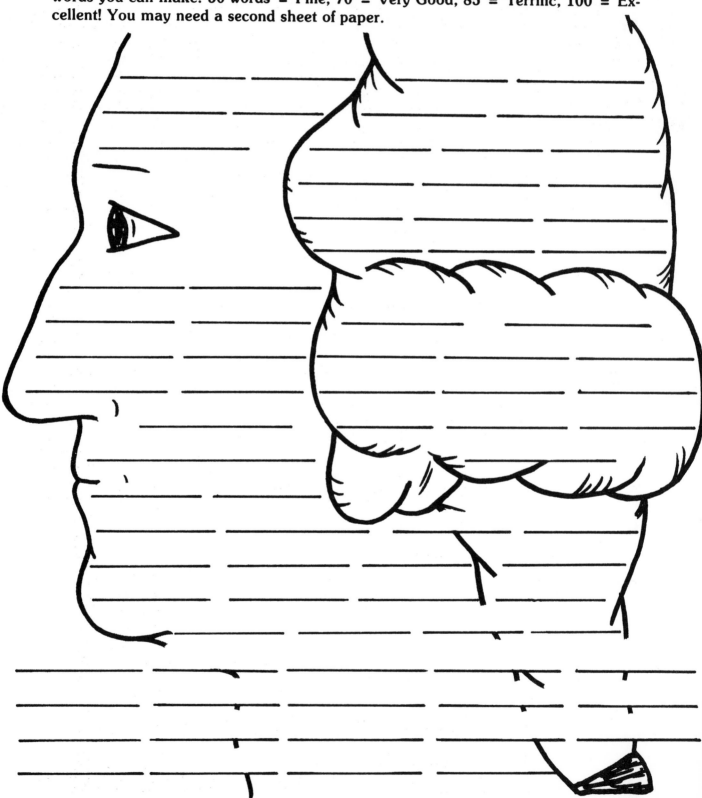

ANIMALS

Animals are among the most refreshing and fascinating things in our world. Children are interested in a variety of animals, their habits and characteristics. These word games encourage creative fluency and flexibility, teach some new words, and familiarize students with the spelling of many animal names. Students can also visit a nearby zoo, interview a veterinarian, draw pictures to illustrate the combination animals they name, make word mine lists from the longer combination names, use animal names for spelling words, and write animal stories for younger children and put them in animal-shaped books. You can discuss with them why animals play such a central role in fables and fairy tales, and which characteristics we associate with various animals are fact or fiction (dirty pigs, sly foxes, etc.).

ANIMAL
WORD SEARCH

You will find thirty-eight animals hidden in the puzzle below. They read up and down ↕ , forward and backward ↔ . Check each one off the list as you find it.

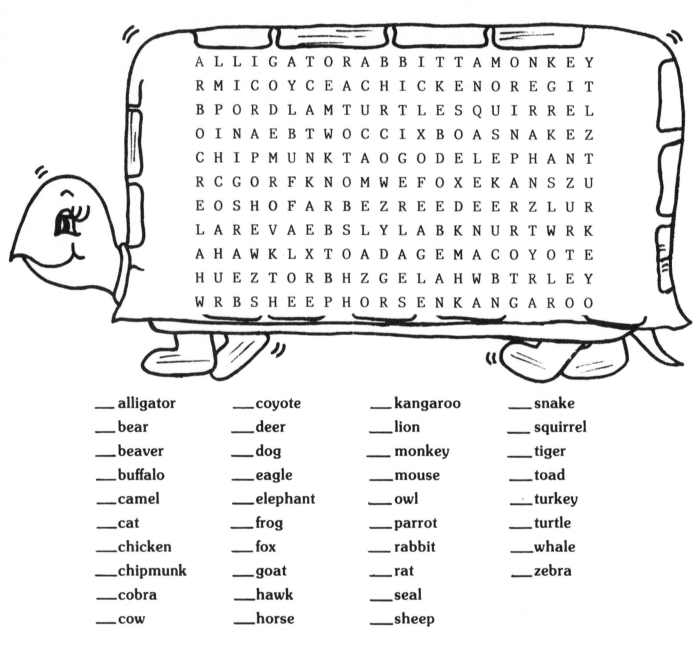

```
A L L I G A T O R A B B I T T A M O N K E Y
R M I C O Y C E A C H I C K E N O R E G I T
B P O R D L A M T U R T L E S Q U I R R E L
O I N A E B T W O C C I X B O A S N A K E Z
C H I P M U N K T A O G O D E L E P H A N T
R C G O R F K N O M W E F O X E K A N S Z U
E O S H O F A R B E Z R E E D E E R Z L U R
L A R E V A E B S L Y L A B K N U R T W R K
A H A W K L X T O A D A G E M A C O Y O T E
H U E Z T O R B H Z G E L A H W B T R L E Y
W R B S H E E P H O R S E N K A N G A R O O
```

__ alligator   __ coyote   __ kangaroo   __ snake
__ bear   __ deer   __ lion   __ squirrel
__ beaver   __ dog   __ monkey   __ tiger
__ buffalo   __ eagle   __ mouse   __ toad
__ camel   __ elephant   __ owl   __ turkey
__ cat   __ frog   __ parrot   __ turtle
__ chicken   __ fox   __ rabbit   __ whale
__ chipmunk   __ goat   __ rat   __ zebra
__ cobra   __ hawk   __ seal
__ cow   __ horse   __ sheep

Which seven animals can you find in the puzzle more than once? _____

_____

80

More Animals

This puzzle has fifty animals hidden in all directions - up and down ↕, forward and backward ↔, and diagonally ↗ ↘.

```
H A L P A C A M A R E T A E T N A N T E L O P E
I E L L E Z A G R I C A L A O K S H O P I E M N
P N E V A R X T A E W H E S I O R L C O L U E I
P L L A M A Y A U B H S I B L A E P M I C E A P
O A C O U G R C O N U T L M G O R I C A R C B U
P R S E P N O B B I G E N U P J T A W O C T A C
O E A L E M A O K L M O O A C A N H E M R D S R
T O R N V D I B Y U U C R B P C N S A H O O E O
A P E N G U I N R K S D I I E K A Z S A C L R P
M A U E I U X W K A S S R E L A G X E T O P U X
U N R M P L T O R T O I S E G L W O L E D H T F
S E A B A T B A U N P R W O M B A T I E I L L
X Y R S K U N K N U O B I R A C S R O H L N U O
R H I N O C E R O S R E E D N I E R N C E A V W
```

___ alpaca	___emu	___ marmoset	___raven
___ anteater	___gazelle	___ mink	___reindeer
___ antelope	___ gibbon	___okapi	___rhinoceros
___ badger	___ gnu	___ opossum	___skunk
___ bison	___gorilla	___ orangutan	___sloth
___ bobcat	___hippopotamus	___oryx	___tapir
___ caribou	___hyena	___ostrich	___tortoise
___ cheetah	___jackal	___ panther	___vulture
___ chimpanzee	___koala	___pelican	___weasel
___ cougar	___lemur	___penguin	___wolf
___ crocodile	___leopard	___porcupine	___wombat
___ dolphin	___llama	___puma	
___ elk	___lynx	___raccoon	

Other animals in this puzzle _____

_____

How Many Animals Can you List?

Put your brain to work! Think of as many animals as you can, and write them on this page. First do it by yourself; then make a second list with one or two partners. While writing your lists, be sure to include unusual animals others won't use.

_____ _____ _____ _____
_____ _____ _____ _____
_____ _____ _____ _____
_____ _____ _____ _____
_____ _____ _____ _____
_____ _____ _____ _____
_____ _____ _____ _____
_____ _____ _____ _____
_____ _____ _____ _____
_____ _____ _____ _____
_____ _____ _____ _____
_____ _____ _____ _____
_____ _____ _____ _____
_____ _____ _____ _____
_____ _____ _____ _____
_____ _____ _____ _____
_____ _____ _____ _____

You might want to group your animals in categories, such as mammals, birds, reptiles, amphibians, fish, marsupials, insects, etc.

Find the Animals

Fill in the blank in each word to complete the name of an animal or group of animals. Then transfer that letter to the box beside it. If your letters are correct there will be eleven animal names reading down in the boxes.

1. TUR_LE
    GOR_LLA
    COU_AR
    CHE_TAH
    LEOPA_D

2. CHI_KEN
    GI_AFFE
    R_BIN
    BOB_AT
    W_LF
    GOL_FISH
    B_RD
    BUFFA_O
    SH_EP

3. REIN_EER
    T_AD
    S_OTH
    CHI_MUNK
    _AWK
    PENGU_N
    I_SECT

4. TU_KEY
    WH_LE
    RHINO_EROS
    JA_KAL
    D_LPHIN
    LI_N
    PO_Y

5. PELI_AN
    PANT_ER
    F_SH
    MA_MAL
    O_OSSUM
    BE_R
    G_U
    GA_ELLE
    WEAS_L
    CAM_L

6. ALLI_ATOR
    WOMB_T
    _EBRA
    N_WT
    KOA_A
    WA_RUS
    RAV_N

7. ELEP_ANT
    MOSQU_TO
    ANTELO_E
    PROCU_INE
    H_RSE
    MARSU_IAL
    F_X
    S_ORK
    LL_MA
    A_PHIBIAN
    B_TTERFLY
    MOU_E

8. OSTRI_H
    FR_G
    L_NX
    BIS_N
    TOR_OISE
    R_PTILE

9. CATT_E
    B_AVER
    PARR_T
    HI_PO
    GO_T
    COB_A
    BA_GER

10. MO_H
    P_PPY
    ZEB_A
    MUS_RAT
    KITT_N
    H_ENA

11. PEAC_CK
    SHA_K
    R_CCOON
    S_AKE
    KAN_AROO
    SK_NK
    VUL_URE
    R_BBIT
    MO_KEY

83

Hidden Animals

The name of an animal is hidden in each sentence. It is not one of the obvious animal names used, and it may be hidden inside one or several words. Can you find each one?

1. Please allow plenty of time to see all the shows at the zoo.

2. We saw a walrus named Bob catch a ball on his nose.

3. Bob then threw the ball to a seal named Adolph in the next pool.

4. The penguin act came later in the show.

5. Water animals move with awkwardness on land.

6. The fuzzy monkey wore a cap each time he ran across the stage.

7. I am still amazed at the tricks the animals learned!

8. As the running mother lion began to pant, her pace slowed.

There are *two* animals hidden in each of these sentences. Look carefully!

1. The new car I bought stands out in a crowd.

2. An artist was painting a lemur on a large yellow easel.

3. Cleo, pardon me, please, so I can see the elephant better.

4. The new set of china bowls arrived yesterday in a large wooden crate.

5. The millionaire had gold faucet handles put on his sink and bathtub.

6. The clown shouted, "I'll make the balloon go 'bang' or I'll arrange a new trick!"

7. When my brother, Bob, is on Santa's lap he always promises to be a really good boy.

8. As Mom drove into the parking slot her ears picked up what seemed to be a very strange noise in the engine.

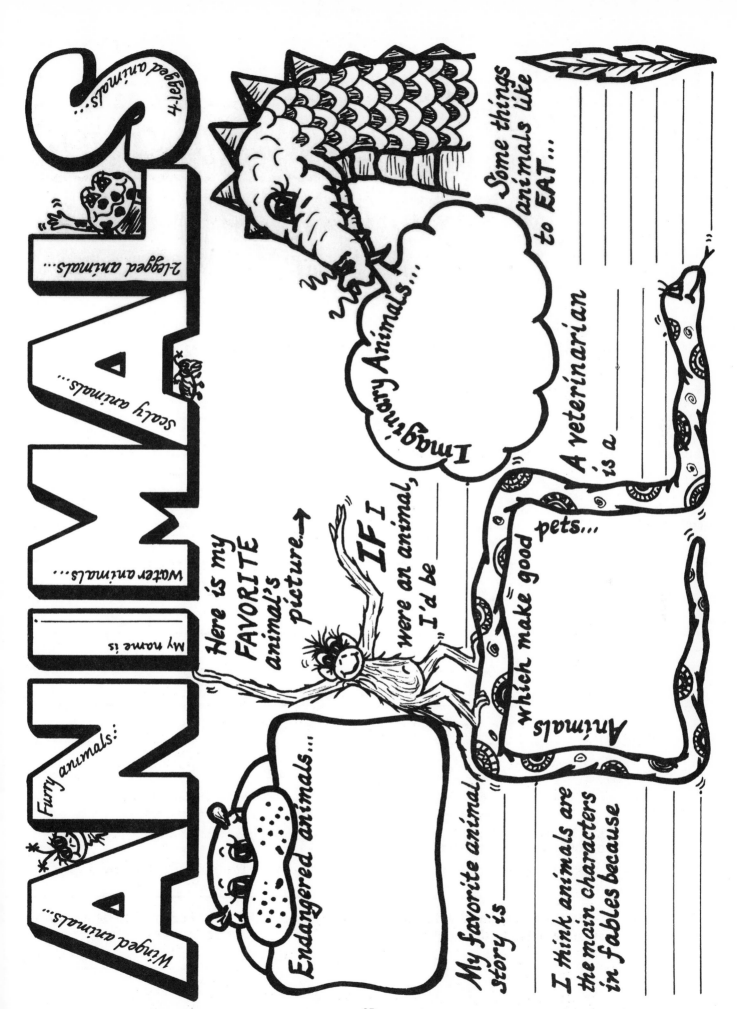

ANIMALS

+Legged animals...

2-Legged animals...

Scaly animals...

Water animals...

My name is _____

Fury animals:

Winged animals...

Here is my FAVORITE animal's picture→

Imaginary Animals...

I IF I were an animal, I'd be _____

My favorite animal story is _____

Endangered animals...

Some things animals like to EAT...

A veterinarian is a _____

Animals which make good pets...

I think animals are the main characters in fables because _____

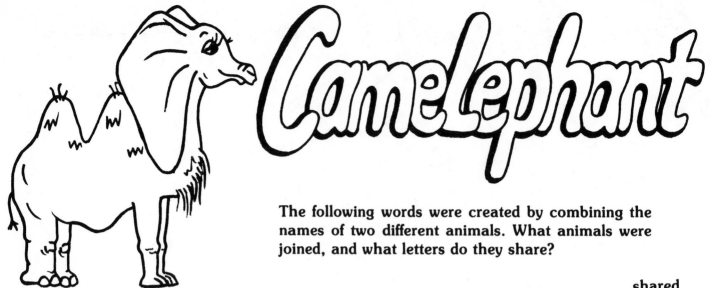

CameLephant

The following words were created by combining the names of two different animals. What animals were joined, and what letters do they share?

	ANIMAL #1	ANIMAL #2	shared letters
1. camelephant	camel	elephant	el
2. rhinocerostrich			
3. pantheron			
4. turtleopard			
5. apeel			
6. kangarooster			
7. goldfishark			
8. ostrichimpanzee			
9. cormoranteater			
10. antelopelican			
11. constrictortoise			
12. zebrattler			

Who were combined to create these words?

godzillama			
buffalorax			
hulkangaroo			

86

More Animal Combinations

cardinal   seal   hippopotamus   fox

muskrat   peacock   leopard   giraffe

cobra   gerbil   antelope   okapi

camel   squirrel   rabbit   badger

ferret   cow   alligator   elk

oriole   oxen   pig   chicken

ostrich   alpaca   elephant   owl

New Name	Animal #1	Animal #2	shared letters

Collective Nouns

Collective nouns are words used to describe a group of things - a *class* of students, a *crowd* of people. Below are some collective nouns used to group animals. Use the list to fill in the blanks in the sentences. YOU WILL NEED TO ADD THE PREPOSITION "OF" BEFORE EACH NOUN.

a *host* of locusts   a *pitying* of doves
a *murder* of crows   a *rookery* of seals
a *murmuration* of starlings a *skulk* of foxes
a *nye* of pheasants   a *sloth* of bears
an *ostentation* of peacocks a *troop* of kangaroos

1. We awoke to the cooing of a large pitying_____ in the nearby trees.

2. The ripening corn brought a murder_____ to the farmer's meadow.

3. The number of tracks around the opening among the old tree's roots told us it was the home of a skulk _____.

4. The farmers hoped the cloud looming on the horizon was not a host _____.

5. When we were in Yellowstone National Park last summer, a sloth _____ visited our camp every night to raid the garbage cans.

6. A murmuration _____ settled on the telephone lines along our street last night.

7. The eerie cries in the evening came from the ostentation _____ in the garden.

8. On our trip to the Australian "Out Back," our guide helped us sneak up on several troops _____ camped among the eucalyptus groves.

9. A rookery _____ covered the rocks near the beach at low tide.

10. We used to see a nye _____ on the drive to town before the hunting season began.

88

Collective Nouns

Use the collective nouns listed below to fill in the blanks in the sentences. Be sure to add "*of*" before the noun - a swarm *of* bees.

an *aerie* of eagles
an *army* of herring
a *bale* of turtles
a *clowder* of cats
a *crash* of rhinoceroses

a *drey* of squirrels
an *exaltation* of larks
a *flight* of swallows
a *gam* of whales
a *gang* of elk

1. The members of the zoo expedition built a strong fence around their camp to keep out the crash_____ they were studying.

2. With the coming of spring, an exaltation _____ moved into our town.

3. We had to use binoculars to spot the aerie_____ high on the cliff.

4. We took the cruise from San Diego in hopes of seeing a gam _____ on its annual migration.

5. The fishermen aboard the fishing boats were surprised to find an army _____ _____ so far out at sea.

6. The oak tree in our yard produces enough acorns to feed a drey _____ _____ during the winter.

7. We drove over the crest of the mountain and saw a gang _____ in the meadow below.

8. All the little noises from the closet told us we now had a clowder _____ in the house.

9. People travel from everywhere to watch the first flight _____ return to San Juan Capistrano in March each year.

10. Spring arrived at the pond and revealed a new bale _____.

More Animal Groups

Think up some sentences of your own using some of the collective nouns listed below.

a *colony* of ants
a *drove* of hogs (a *sounder* of swine)
a *gaggle* of geese (a *skein* of geese in flight)
a *herd* of zebras
a *hover* of trout
a *hurtle* of sheep

a *pack* of dogs
a *pride* of lions
a *school* of fish (a *shoal* of fish)
a *trip* of goats
an *unkindness* of ravens
a *warren* of rabbits

_____

_____

_____

_____

_____

_____

_____

_____

_____

_____

_____

_____

_____

_____

_____

_____

There is a great deal of interest in sports, games and exercising in our society. You can create a high level of motivation and encourage learning through total body involvement by using sports activities in your classroom. These word games may be of special interest to students who are athletically inclined, or those who prefer to be spectators.

Students can also read biographies of famous sports personalities, interview local TV sportscasters and game announcers, take a class trip to a sporting event, have magic circle/group discussions about sports attitudes and how we react to them, make sports scrapbooks, create games for the future, and respond to weekly graffiti boards on sports topics (for example, "How many sports/games do you know?" "I like to play...," "Tools and equipment used in sports...").

Sports Scramble

Scrambled words are a challenge to your vocabulary. Can you unscramble these letters to find names of sports?

SOME TEAM SPORTS

1. aloftolb _____
2. heyock _____
3. lalovelybl _____
4. croesc _____
5. ablesalb _____
6. lostblaf _____
7. midnobtan _____

WATER SPORTS

1. griwon _____
2. rusfnig _____
3. figinsh _____
4. wmigmisn _____
5. givind _____
6. nibogat _____
7. eatwr igiksn _____
8. glisnai _____
9. hganiytc _____

YOU CAN DO THESE SPORTS BY YOURSELF OR WITH OTHERS

1. dotsibkranega _____
2. flog _____
3. ungrinn _____
4. thewig fgniitl _____
5. ihngik _____
6. myscatsing _____
7. glowbin _____
8. gclicny _____
9. carhrye _____

OTHER SPORTS

1. craing _____
2. sinent _____
3. gunhint _____
4. ladalbnh _____
5. nogixb _____

If you are stumped, look for "ing," as in "surfing."

Sports Scramble #2

This page is for major leaguers...or those with a sports book! Good luck!

TRACK & FIELD

1. toscyncorusr _____
2. sudics _____
3. lugnihdr _____
4. loep gvtanlui _____
5. njeavil oghwtnri _____

TEAM SPORTS

1. slabltekab _____
2. burgy _____
3. tarew oolp _____
4. lesdapebl _____
5. clsoaser _____

WITH ANIMALS

1. kshbocear gdrnii _____
2. odg cirnga _____

ALWAYS OUTDOORS

1. imnanotu lgbinicm _____
2. nusgnikelp _____
3. wlan bgnolwi _____

IN THE AIR

1. ysk giinvd _____
2. ngah diinggl _____
3. oth rai loogbinianl _____

WINTER SPORTS

1. singik _____
2. cei tgsanik _____
3. epdes kgtsnai _____
4. isk mugnjip _____
5. noibwsglonim _____
6. dolbigbedns _____

MORE SPORTS

1. gngiojg _____
2. lsnegiwtr _____
3. lorrel ktnsaig _____
4. bitmulgn _____
5. cinfgen _____
6. grad cgrnai _____

If you are stumped, turn

Games People Play

Can you find the forty-two games people play that are hidden in this puzzle?

```
J S K A T E B O A R D I N G S W I M M I N G H
A P O G Y M A S F I S H Q U I R Y G L I D N O
V E J F C I S X O B I O C R N E A S B X S I R
E L O W T N E Y O R N S Y B N S C U A O N B S
L U G A L B B R T A I K C A E T H R D B O M E
I N G T E G A W B D T E L S T L T F M X W I B
N K N E U K L L A N M Y I K N I I I I D M L A
T I I R S H L A L A C R N E G N N N N I O C C
H N D S G A U C L O H S G T O G G G T V B N K
R G I K N N S R A Q U E T B A L L G O I I I R
O N L I I D O O D G N I G A K S R N N N L A I
W I G I L B C S Y L T N W L H I K I N G I T D
I G G N B A C S K I I N G L Y E K C O H N N I
N G N G M L E E S W N N O G N I T A O B G U N
G O A M U L R J O G G O G W A T E R P O L O G
N J H O T A I R B A L L O O N I N G O L F M I
I S C I T S A N M Y G N I T A K S D E E P S K
```

hot air ballooning   mountain climbing

badminton	football	horseback riding	jogging	softball
baseball	golf	hang gliding	lacrosse	surfing
basketball	gymnastics	javelin throwing	racing	swimming
boating	handball	skateboarding	rowing	tennis
boxing	hiking	snowmobiling	rugby	tumbling
cycling	hockey	speed skating	skating	water polo
discus	hunting	spelunking	skiing	wrestling
diving	hurdling	water skiing	soccer	yachting

94

Baseball Word Mine Game

HOW TO PLAY: The object of this game is to see how many words you can make using the letters on the baseball field below. Each word must have two or more letters. You can use each letter only once per word.

HOW TO SCORE: Each word counts as one base, and four words equal a run. Find your score by dividing your total number of words by four. If you wish you can keep words with 5 or more letters in a special column and count as a home run.

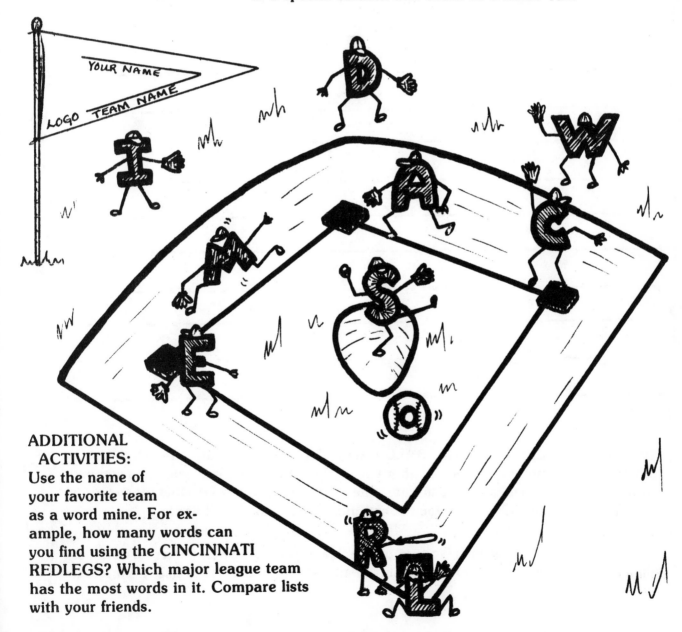

ADDITIONAL ACTIVITIES: Use the name of your favorite team as a word mine. For example, how many words can you find using the CINCINNATI REDLEGS? Which major league team has the most words in it. Compare lists with your friends.

BATTER UP! Here are your letters.

SCORE :

S L A C E M I D W O R

_____ _____ _____ _____ _____

_____ _____ _____ _____ _____

_____ _____ _____ _____ _____

_____ _____ _____ _____ _____

_____ _____ _____ _____ _____

_____ _____ _____ _____ _____

_____ _____ _____ _____ _____

_____ _____ _____ _____ _____

_____ _____ _____ _____ _____

_____ _____ _____ _____ _____

_____ _____ _____ _____ _____

_____ _____ _____ _____ _____

_____ _____ _____ _____ _____

OPTIONAL RULES FOR BASEBALL FANS: Try your hand at managing! Use a pinch hitter to improve your score after you've thought up as many words as you can with those on the field now. Substitute a new letter for the batter. How many words can you add? Remember, once you substitute, you cannot use R again.

TO PLAY ANOTHER GAME: Go to your bench and substitute new letters for some or all of those now in the game. Once you substitute, remember not to use the original letters.

Whether you eat to live, or live to eat, food is a basic need we are all concerned with daily. It is a subject we are all familiar with and have definite ideas and preferences about. Food can be a social activity and an avenue for much versatile learning and pleasure. These word games include personal reactions to food, brainstorming, unscrambling words, finding words in puzzles, and categorizing some foreign foods. Additional food activities can include writing recipes, making a class cookbook, making a meal in class, gathering menus from local restaurants from which students create math problems involving eating out, imaginary trips to the grocery store, designing an ideal kitchen or dining area, and creating food for the future.

FOOD WORDS

This apple has at least fifty words around its edge. Follow the arrows without skipping any letters, and see how many words you can find. For example, at the top left is ORANGE, which has other words in it. There are eighteen food words and at least thirty-two others. 40 = Good, 45 = Very Good, 50 or more = Excellent

YAMORANGESHAMBURGERICEGGPLANTACORNUTOMATOWATERMELONIONSTRAWBERRIESHERBETY

98

FOOD

Everyday I eat...

At lunchtime I eat...

Food makes me...

I like food because...

If I could have ANYTHING for dinner, I'd choose...

Food is important to us all because

Things I like to drink...

Words we use to describe food

The four basic food groups are

My Favorite Recipe

Ingredients:

Directions:

Other foods I like

Design a brand new kind of food! Describe it & draw its package.

People in other countries sometimes eat different food because

RIGHT NOW... I would like to eat...

What 4 things do our taste buds really taste?

This page was done by

Scrambled Food

Unscramble the letters of these foods. Some have more than one word.

1. remaubrgh _____
2. crniefsrhef _____
3. gatihestp _____
4. cirobloc _____
5. kesat _____
6. otedapseakotb _____
7. gesg _____
8. pskropcoh _____
9. ardeb _____
10. ehesec _____
11. etwespoestaot _____
12. pascut _____
13. kicnehc _____
14. namoedel _____
15. spelap _____

16. tupatebnretu _____
17. ropnocp _____
18. shogtod _____
19. mah _____
20. izapz _____
21. sangero _____
22. aldas _____
23. voilari _____
24. acormina _____
25. kmil _____
26. starocr _____
27. cepaseh _____
28. rudstam _____
29. sockeoi _____
30. aronlag _____

Make up scrambled foods of your own, and let a friend unscramble them.

_____
_____

100

ALPHABET FOOD

How many foods can you list that start with each letter (except X) of the alphabet?

1-2 words = 1 point each; 3-4 = 2 points; 5-7 = 3 points; 8 = 4 points.
BONUS POINTS: 4 each for words beginning with I, J, K, Q, V, and Y; 10 for U and Z.

60 = OK , Keep thinking, 75 = Good, 90 = Very Good, 110 or more = Excellent

A_____

B_____

C_____

D_____

E_____

F_____

G_____

H_____

I_____

J_____

K_____

L_____

M_____

N_____

O_____

P_____

Q_____

R_____

S_____

T_____

U_____

V_____

W_____

Y_____

Z_____

International Food

Categorize each food according to its national origin.

egg foo yong
lasagne
tacos
barbequed ribs
Peking duck
chile rellenos

burritos
quesadillas
hot dogs
spaghetti
baked ham
cioppino

veal scallopini
turkey and dressing
sweet and sour pork
eggplant parmigiana
turkey tetrazzini
fried rice

fried chicken
won tons
tamales
tostadas
stir fry

enchiladas
ravioli
steak
egg rolls
hamburgers

American

_____
_____
_____
_____
_____
_____
_____

Mexican

_____
_____
_____
_____
_____
_____
_____

Italian

_____
_____
_____
_____
_____
_____

Chinese

_____
_____
_____
_____
_____
_____

Kitchen Utensils

List all the utensils, tools and items in a kitchen that have to do with food, its storage, preparation, eating, etc.

What's Cooking?

This puzzle contains at least sixty words related to the preparation and cooking of food. The words are hidden forward and backward, up and down, and diagonally. If you know what all these words mean, you are on your way to being a good cook!

```
P R E P A R E W I S K M A R I N A T E N
U A H I G H O C M A S E L K C I P I S I
R G R I L L A A S T E A M E D I U M A A
E K A B O N E R S E A S O N S T E E E R
E T S A O R B Y R K S U P E E L E T R D
B N Y E C I D R C O R R E C T C S I G E
A I R O V A L F O M L E H A U A C O A R
R A F R L I O R B S T O L A B E A T E H
B R N C O O K I E U P R S D A E R P S S
E T A R Y R F T A P E E D N E L B I D
Q S P O A C H S O F T B O I L R A S M N
U E N I B M O C H I L L T F I S X I M I
E X W A H T L I O B D R A H T I M B E R
G R A T E W A S H R E P R E H E A T R G
```

___prepare	___blend	___drain	___season	___bake	___panfry
___chop	___rice	___chill	___correct	___broil	___deep-fat fry
___grate	___whip	___heat	___flavor	___grill	___barbeque
___dice	___beat	___time	___smoke	___roast	___hard-boil
___puree	___spread	___high	___can	___steam	___soft-boil
___grind	___thaw	___medium	___pickle	___boil	___stir-fry
___sift	___mix	___low	___baste	___cream	___simmer
___peel	___wisk	___cool	___saute	___poach	___measure
___wash	___add	___grease	___melt	___broast	___preheat
___shred	___combine	___strain	___parboil	___sauce	___marinate

HOUSES

The desire for a comfortable place to live is something we all share. The word games and activities in this chapter deal with types of homes, the people who build them, what we put in houses, how we care for them and how we'd choose our dream house to be. Children have all had experience with houses which will help them work these pages successfully. The chapter is designed to stretch the mind beyond our usual limits of vision. Perhaps a picture will form in one child's mind which will create a totally new future environment.

In conjunction with these pages, students can design dream homes, design living environments in space, build models, visit building sites and model homes in the community, learn some math or other skills used by architects and builders, interview speakers from housing, real estate and interior decorating fields, and visit a high school class involved in related studies.

Places to Live

Here are twenty-six anagrams for places to live. Some of them may not be the kinds of places you would choose to make your home, but people have lived in them all. Unscramble the words, then answer the question at the bottom of the page.

1. suoeh _____

2. rilater _____

3. monidincoum _____

4. snoamin _____

5. gawimw _____

6. natemrapt _____

7. lecapa _____

8. sfruomeha _____

9. logoi _____

10. binca _____

11. chnar _____

12. tlaf _____

13. tuh _____

14. tirecornaela civehel _____

15. lestac _____

16. ownt euhos _____

17. mafera _____

18. catrt ehmo _____

19. eetpe _____

20. puledx _____

21. tagoetc _____

22. nyatsh _____

23. letoh _____

24. kasch _____

25. degol _____

26. tnte _____

If you could live in ANY of these places, which one would you choose, and why?

_____

_____

Housework

List all the tools, implements, and materials you can think of that we use (or could use) in the cleaning and maintaining of our homes inside and out.

15 = OK, keep thinking
25 = Good
35 = Very Good
50 or more = Excellent

Home Building Specialists

Can you find the job titles listed on the following page? Check off each one as you find it in the word search puzzle.

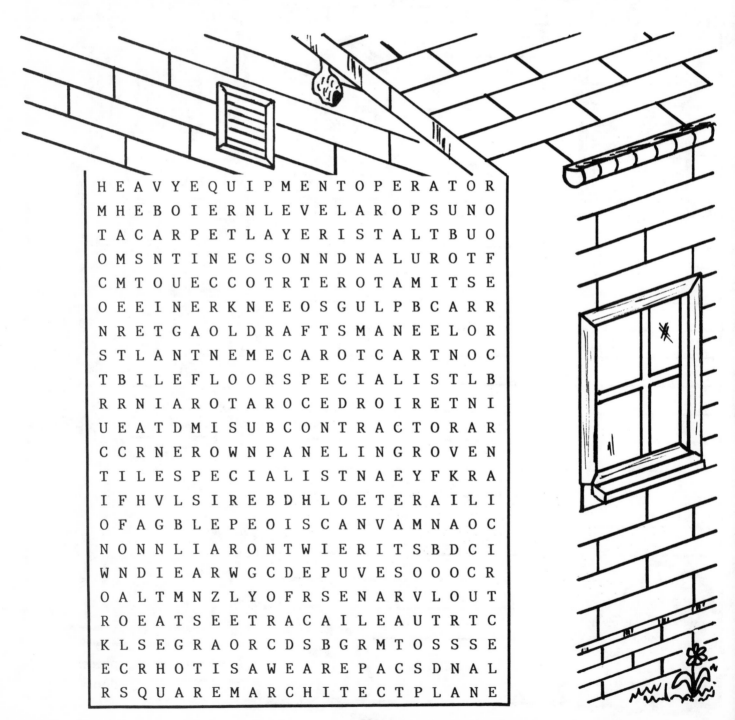

```
H E A V Y E Q U I P M E N T O P E R A T O R
M H E B O I E R N L E V E L A R O P S U N O
T A C A R P E T L A Y E R I S T A L T B U O
O M S N T I N E G S O N N D N A L U R O T F
C M T O U E C C O T R T E R O T A M I T S E
O E E I N E R K N E E O S G U L P B C A R R
N R E T G A O L D R A F T S M A N E E L O R
S T L A N T N E M E C A R O T C A R T N O C
T B I L E F L O O R S P E C I A L I S T L B
R R N I A R O T A R O C E D R O I R E T N I
U E A T D M I S U B C O N T R A C T O R A R
C C R N E R O W N P A N E L I N G R O V E N
T I L E S P E C I A L I S T N A E Y F K R A
I F H V L S I R E B D H L O E T E R A I L I
O F A G B L E P E O I S C A N V A M N A O C
N O N N L I A R O N T W I E R I T S B D C I
W N D I E A R W G C D E P U V E S O O O C R
O A L T M N Z L Y O F R S E N A R V L O U T
R O E A T S E E T R A C A I L E A U T R T C
K L S E G R A O R C D S B G R M T O S S S E
E C R H O T I S A W E A R E P A C S D N A L
R S Q U A R E M A R C H I T E C T P L A N E
```

HOME BUILDING SPECIALISTS

__ architect
__ draftsman
__ contractor
__ loan officer
__ estimator
__ surveyor
__ subcontractor
__ heavy equipment operator
__ laborer
__ construction worker
__ plumber
__ mason
__ carpenter
__ electrician

__ heating/ventilation
__ roofer
__ shingler
__ glazer
__ floor specialist
__ drywaller
__ plasterer
__ cabinet maker
__ tile specialist
__ painter
__ landscaper
__ gardner
__ carpet layer
__ interior decorator

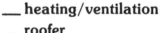

EXTRA: Some materials and tools

__ steel
__ brick
__ cement
__ glass
__ wood
__ pipe
__ stucco
__ shingle
__ paneling
__ wire
__ trim
__ tile
__ handles

__ hammer
__ tractor
__ saw
__ plane
__ level
__ square
__ nails
__ screws
__ bolts
__ nuts
__ plugs
__ doors

What's Inside?

How many things can you name inside different rooms in a house? Take an inventory of your house (or any home) and list all the things in the rooms below. Use paper if you need more space.

living room	kitchen

bedroom	bathroom

On another sheet of paper you might list things found in one or more of these rooms: playroom, library, guest room, basement, laundry room, attic, den, study, garage.

Just Imagine...

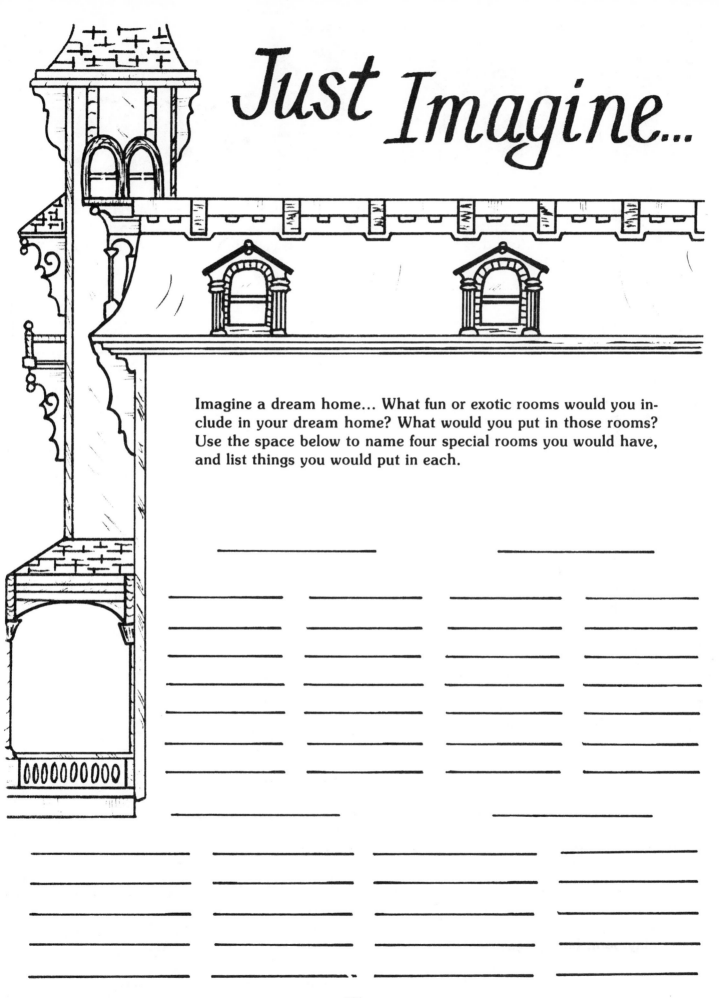

Imagine a dream home... What fun or exotic rooms would you include in your dream home? What would you put in those rooms? Use the space below to name four special rooms you would have, and list things you would put in each.

Most of the places listed below house a variety of animals. List *different* animals which might inhabit each place. If you have more ideas, use another sheet of paper. There are a few spaces for other houses you may know. If you are not familiar with any of these places, look them up in the dictionary.

BARN	HOLE	POND	OCEAN
STABLE	BURROW	AQUARIUM	LAKE
CORRAL	DEN	CAGE	TIDE POOL
PEN	NEST	COOP	HOUSE
WARREN	HIVE	STY	
WEB	DAM	LAIR	

Here are some holiday ideas to add to your files. These activities are designed for creative thought, amusement and word practice. Perhaps these ideas will encourage you or your students to create new holiday games and puzzles. You can add word shapes for Halloween and Easter, word search puzzles, word mine activities with "Merry Christmas," and mental exercises for other holidays. One fun activity that can accompany these is making up a new holiday! What might it represent? Where would it be celebrated, and when? What special events would take place that day? Would there be family get-togethers and gift exchanges? What special food would be prepared and eaten? How about creating a world-wide holiday?

LABOR DAY

In most states of the United States, the first Monday in September is set aside as a legal holiday called Labor Day. This holiday honors the important part working people play in our society. How many different types of jobs can you list? Below are some categories to help you get started. Use another sheet of paper when you need more space.

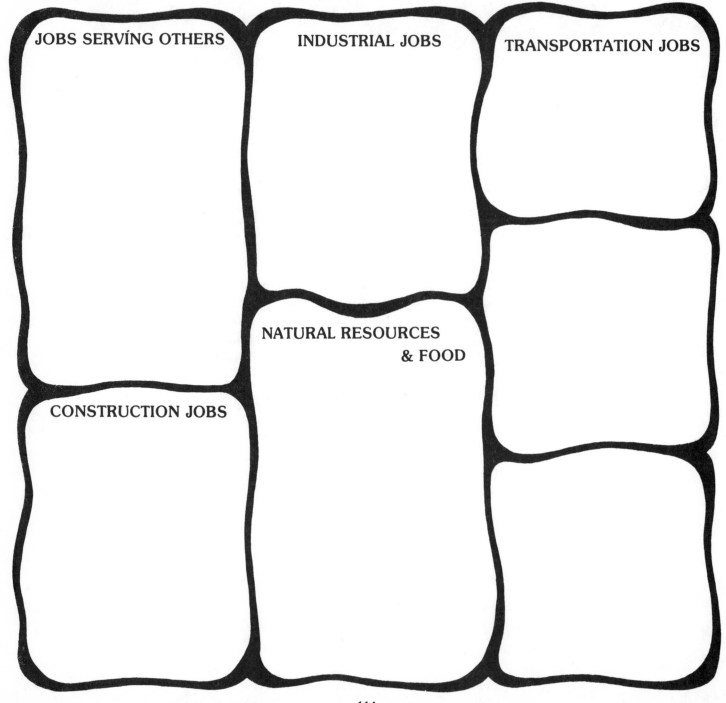

JOBS SERVING OTHERS

INDUSTRIAL JOBS

TRANSPORTATION JOBS

NATURAL RESOURCES & FOOD

CONSTRUCTION JOBS

Adjectives are words that describe or tell about nouns. By writing a different adjective in each of the blanks below you can create an interesting story. Read this story through first, then create a Halloween atmosphere through your descriptive words. Do not use any adjective more than once. After you fill all the blanks, give your story a title.

_____

The _____ moon was shining down on the _____, _____ house. Its _____ gate, _____ fence, and _____ windows make it look like a _____ home. The _____ building was sagging, and the _____ roof had several _____ holes in it.

Through the _____ windows, you could see _____ furniture and _____ curtains. In one _____ corner, a(n) _____ spider had built a _____, _____ web. There were _____ carpets on the _____ floor, and a _____ lampshade covered a _____ lightbulb. _____ napkins still remained at places around a(n) _____, _____ table. _____ chairs were pushed back from the table as if someone had just finished a _____ meal.

Suddenly a _____ breeze rustled through the _____ room. _____ noises came from the _____ curtains moving in the _____ breeze. The spider's _____ web swayed, and the _____ hinges on the _____ shutters creaked and groaned. A _____ flash of lightning lit up the _____ scene. _____ thunder followed, causing the _____ house to quiver. A _____ bolt of lightning screeched through the _____ night, hit the _____ house, and set it on fire. The _____ flames illuminated the _____ countryside for miles around. In a matter of minutes, the _____ house burned to the ground.

HALLOWEEN

This word search puzzle has fifty-two fun and grotesque words hidden in it. Can you find them in the caldron?

```
F R A N K E N S T E I N G H O U L S
A U H A U N T Y R A C S O O Z E S I
N O N I G H T D H O W L B R O O M M
T N A I G Z Y N R F E I L R L W O A
A U T N A G R A G R G T I O Z N S G
S E M U T S O C N E N H N R S P N I
Y P E E R C G O I A A E S T E K R N
G O R P A N I C N K R R E L K E E A
R G O U A P P L E S T R L A M O T T
O O K E I R H S T G S P O O K A N I
T R I K S A M G H O S T S K E E A O
E D R A C U L A G H A R V E S T L N
S L I M E L A P I W A R L O C K O W
Q U E E R I E W R E M A E R C S K I
U W E R E W O L F U L L M O O N C T
E O P A R T I E S N I K P M U P A C
T R I C K O R T R E A T C A T S J H
```

116

___trick or treat
___fantasy
___goblins
___ghouls
___jack-o'-lantern
___pumpkins
___parties
___apples
___candy
___fun
___scary
___harvest
___full moon
___night
___strange
___costumes
___mask
___makeup
___haunt
___creepy
___slither
___panic
___BOO
___eerie
___gory
___slime
___imagination

___monsters
___grotesque
___Dracula
___Frankenstein
___Gargantua
___werewolf
___frightening
___fearsome
___horror
___witch
___broom
___cats
___spell
___warlock
___freak
___ogre
___giant

___shriek
___EEK
___pale
___ghost

___howl
___spook
___ooze
___scream

117

R. I. P.
Casket Robbers
32 FLAVORS

Create thirty-two freaky, frightful flavors of ice cream to tempt and tame the most horrid Halloween monsters! Use *alliterations* (repeat the beginning sound in each word), and have a beastly good time!

1. Grotesque Gruesome Grape
2. _____
3. _____
4. _____
5. _____
6. _____
7. _____
8. _____
9. _____
10. _____
11. _____
12. _____
13. _____
14. _____
15. _____
16. _____

17. _____
18. _____
19. _____
20. _____
21. _____
22. _____
23. _____
24. _____
25. _____
26. _____
27. _____
28. _____
29. _____
30. _____
31. _____
32. _____

HERE LIES JOHN YEAST.   PARDON ME FOR NOT RISING!

118

Christmas Word Tree

There are forty-six words hidden in this Christmas tree. Follow the arrows clockwise to see if you can find them all. For example, at the top of the tree you will find CHRISTMAS, which has three smaller words within it. Enjoy!

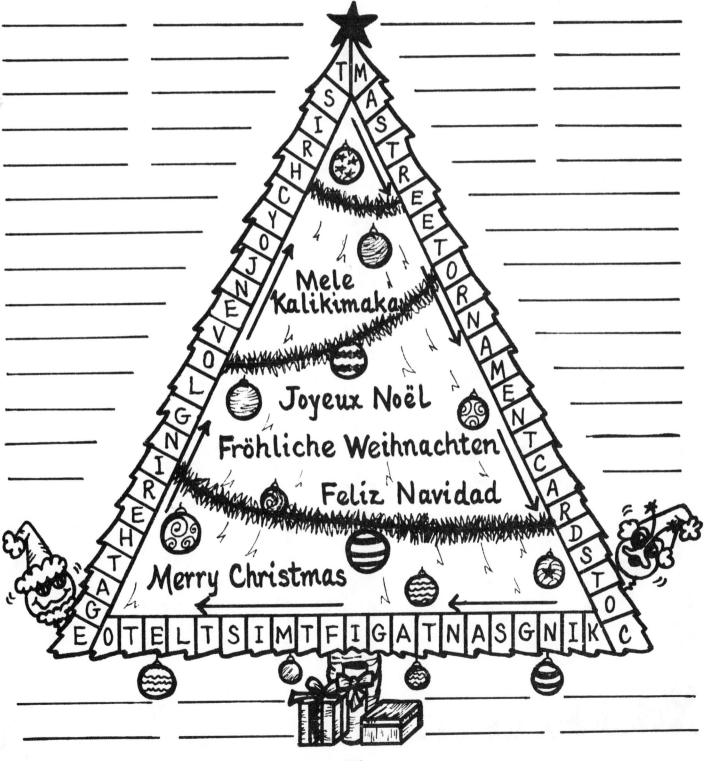

Christmas Thoughts

Put your brain to work thinking of items that will fit these lists. You will need extra paper. Here's how to score your results: 1 point for each answer up to the number requested; 2 points for further items to 20; 3 points each for 21 or more.

1-6 = OK, Keep Thinking, 7-16 = Good, 17-30 = Very Good, 31 or more = Excellent

7 THINGS ON CHRISTMAS TREES

1. _____ 8. _____
2. _____ 9. _____
3. _____ 10. _____
4. _____ 11. _____
5. _____ 12. _____
6. _____ 13. _____
7. _____ 14. _____

7 FOODS WE EAT DURING THE HOLIDAYS

1. _____ 8. _____
2. _____ 9. _____
3. _____ 10. _____
4. _____ 11. _____
5. _____ 12. _____
6. _____ 13. _____
7. _____ 14. _____

8 THINGS TO DO DURING WINTER VACATION

1. _____ 9. _____
2. _____ 10. _____
3. _____ 11. _____
4. _____ 12. _____
5. _____ 13. _____
6. _____ 14. _____
7. _____ 15. _____
8. _____ 16. _____

8 PRESENTS I'D LIKE TO GIVE/RECEIVE THIS YEAR

1. _____ 9. _____
2. _____ 10. _____
3. _____ 11. _____
4. _____ 12. _____
5. _____ 13. _____
6. _____ 14. _____
7. _____ 15. _____
8. _____ 16. _____

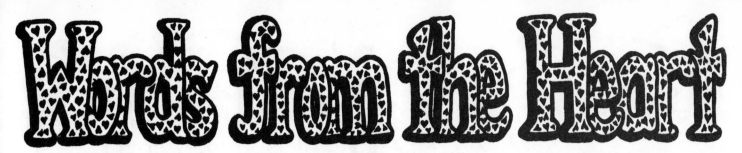

Words from the Heart

There are thirty-six words hidden around this heart. Follow the arrows without skipping any letters, and see if you can find them all. VALENTINES, for example, has five smaller words in it: vale, ale, and tine, plus two more. Write each word in a small heart with the correct number of spaces in it. Have fun!

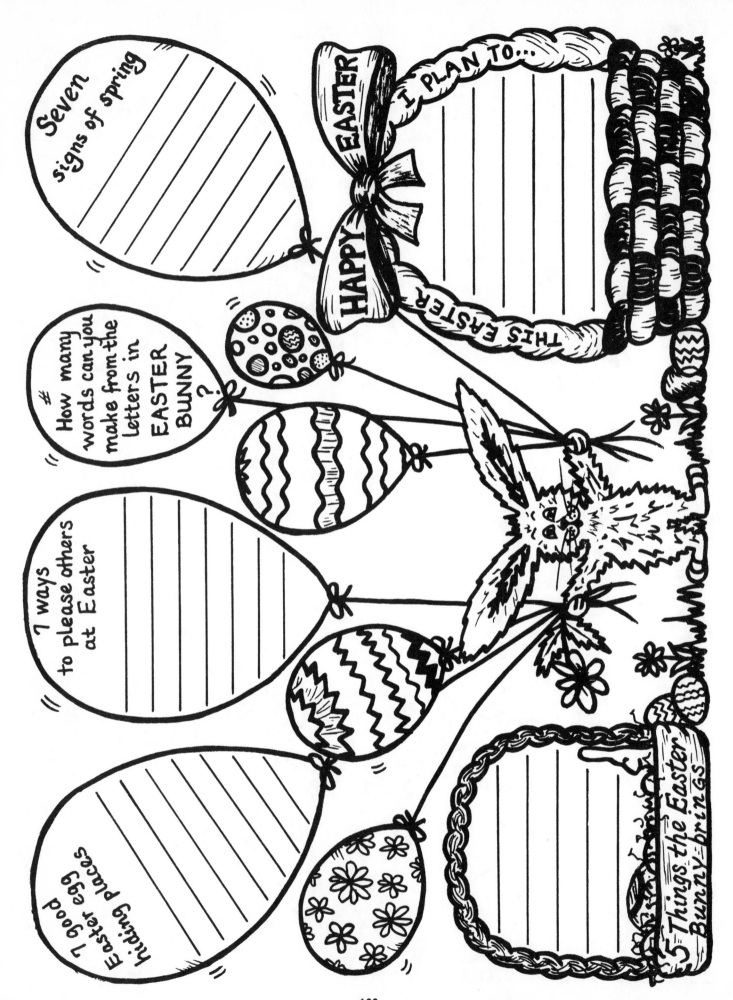

Seven signs of spring

EASTER

HAPPY

I PLAN TO...

THIS EASTER

How many words can you make from the letters in EASTER BUNNY?

7 ways to please others at Easter

7 good Easter egg hiding places

5 Things the Easter Bunny brings

122

More Word Games

SPACE FLIGHT

Challenge your mental computer to find forty-three space age words in this puzzle. After sighting each word, use the data list below for a safety check. Good luck on your mission.

___ manned space flight
___ scientific research
___ space shuttle
___ auxiliary power unit
___ mission control

___ launch site
___ safety checks
___ physical exams
___ communications
___ ground crew
___ astronaut
___ spaceship
___ blast off
___ touchdown

___ atmosphere
___ ignition
___ satellite
___ lift-off
___ hypersonic
___ commander
___ countdown
___ jettison
___ cool down
___ computer

___ Houston
___ Apollo
___ Columbia
___ takeoff
___ cockpit
___ mission
___ voyager
___ docking
___ landing
___ controls

___ flight
___ orbit
___ NASA
___ craft
___ shield
___ tiles
___ pilot
___ data
___ rocket

```
S P A C E S H U T T L E F L I G H T M P C
C O U N D F O V O Y A G E R N O Y U A I O
I R X F O F U R U T I N G I E U P A N L M
E E I F C O S E C O N F D A T A E N N O M
N D L O K T T H Y M N F T I B R O E T U
T N I E I S O U D E A W T O Y A S R D O N
I A A K N A N P O L N C G F T I O T S S I
F M R A G L E M W A N O M E A F N S P K C
I M Y T A B C O N T R O L S G R I A A C A
C O P H Y S I C A L E X A M S A C L C E T
R C O U N T D O W N A I B M U L O C E H I
E O W S H I E L D P I H S E C A P S F C O
S J E T T I S O N T I G N I T I O N L Y N
E G R O U N D C R E W A L C O C K P I T S
A N U A P O L L O K N W O D L O O C G E E
R A N O E L A U N C H S I T E K C U H F L
C S I A L O R T N O C N O I S S I M T A I
H A T M O S P H E R E E T I L L E T A S T
```

124

WEATHER ANAGRAMS

If you can unscramble these weather words, you're hot stuff!

1. mrwa _____
2. dolc _____
3. toh _____
4. lahi _____
5. loco _____
6. ehsnuins _____
7. hnerudt _____
8. ntignligh _____
9. nuropwod _____
10. rotsym _____
11. zidzrel _____
12. dulyoc _____
13. lycilh _____
14. wosn _____
15. snortmows _____
16. etsel _____
17. ystug _____
18. gyofg _____
19. ynidw _____
20. yarni _____
21. yic _____
22. dumih _____
23. mably _____
24. rnegifez _____
25. conleyc _____
26. sractove _____
27. roadton _____
28. rehanucir _____
29. ynophot _____
30. corefast _____
31. razidblz _____
32. trofn _____
33. torper _____
34. rnisatrom _____

125

For a special fee, drivers can now order personalized license plates for their cars. Here is your chance to design some plates FREE! The only limit to your creativity is that each plate has just 7 or 8 spaces for numbers or letters. You can use abbreviations, phonetic spellings, letters like C, R, B, U, and numbers like 2 and 4. RU RED E ? GO 4 IT !!

Oct. CALIFORNIA 1981

IM COOL

ILLINOIS

LAND OF LINCOLN

HINK PINKS

A HINK PINK is a pair of rhyming *one*-syllable words. They are lots of fun and spark your imagination. Here are some examples, and some for you to figure out. Use the blanks to create your own.

an unruly youngster	wild child	an unusual couple	rare pair
second-hand store	swap shop	a fat fish	stout trout
obese feline		tiny sphere	
girl from switzerland		large swine	
large hairpiece		drenched dog	
delighted father		azure church seat	
angry employer			

A HINKY PINKY is a pair of rhyming *two*-syllable words. Can you figure these out?

cautious scholar	prudent student	fancier cardigan	better sweater
happy captain	chipper skipper	ridiculous flower	
thicker serving plate		glass gun	
fake colt		messy duplication	
taller flames		kitchen knife	

A HINKETY PINKETY is a pair of rhyming *three*-syllable words. Challenge your mind by filling in answers, writing descriptions, and making up a new Hinkety Pinkety.

evil preacher	sinister minister	happier dog	merrier terrier
	resident president		crueler jeweler
yearly handbook			

Foreign Languages

This word search puzzle contains the names of fifty-two languages. Because some may be unfamiliar to you, they are only written backward and forward, up and down, Good Luck!

```
P O R T U G U E S E R B O C R O A T I A N
U K D A N I S H Z C B U L G A R I A N I A
N E N G L I S H H E B R E W U T N A B O I
J A R A B I C A I E F M G E R M A N N A D
A N S L O V A K C S I E K L G A E L I C O
B I P O L I S H I M N S O S P A N I S H B
I T A G T H A I D A N E R H C N E R F U M
N A I G E W R O N G I Z E N A I S R E P A
H L A O T I A N A I S K A S U A H C E Z C
S H S I K R U T L N H G N R O M A N I A N
I V I E T N A M E S E S E N I H C Z E C H
D N A I S S U R C J A P A N E S E S I R I
D A U K R A I N I A N U A I L I H A W S N
I T A L I A N M A G Y A R G H M O N G A D
Y N A O M I K S E I R I S A N S K R I T U
H A W A I I A N R U S S I R I S H C T U D
A M H A R I C U L U Z R N O G N I D N A M
S W E D I S H A S H A N T I S F U L A H A
```

___English	___Dutch	___Tagalog	___Polish	___Latin	___Arabic
___Irish	___Danish	___Korean	___Bulgarian	___Hebrew	___Bantu
___Gaelic	___Swedish	___Japanese	___Romanian	___Yiddish	___Swahili
___Welsh	___Finnish	___Vietnamese	___Czeck	___Sanskrit	___Hausa
___Spanish	___Norwegian	___Thai	___Slovak	___Hindu	___Mandingo
___French	___Icelandic	___Laotian	___Serbo-Croatian	___Punjabi	___Amharic
___German	___Eskimoan	___Cambodian	___Magyar	___Burmese	___Zulu
___Italian	___Hawaiian	___Russian	___Turkish	___Fulah	
___Portuguese	___Chinese	___Ukrainian	___Persian	___Ashanti	

Answer Key

HAPPY, SAD OR PEACEFUL   page 5

HAPPY - glad, excited, cheerful, joyful, bright, delighted, inspired, pleased, merry, elated, blissful, ecstatic, jolly, jubilant

SAD - upset, lonely, sorrowful, gloomy, melancholy, unhappy, spiritless, troubled, discouraged, dreary, miserable, disheartened, pensive, solemn

PEACEFUL - relaxed, tranquil, still, unruffled, quiet, calm, mild, settled, restful, composed, content, satisfied, untroubled, gentle

WORD MINES

REPRESENTATIVE   Samples (Can use 2 each - r & t; or e 4 times)   page 13
R - rent, rat, rate, resent, rave, rain, rest, rear, reset, rare, rase, reap, ran, rant, rap, repair, represent, revere, reverse, reverent, reset, ripen, reinvest, rip, restate, repaste, retrain, retape, repent
P - present, pat, pen, pate, pave, pain, pane, pest, peer, pear, pare, pair, past, pan, prevent, paste, part, print, paint, par, pert
S - sent, sate, sane, save, sear, seer, set, state, sieve, serpent, spear, spare, sprint, spent, sprain, stare, stair, stain, start, steer, sap, saint, seep, seat, steep
N - never, nest, nerve, near, nave, native, nap, nape
T - train, tent, trait, tint, tan, tap, test, tear, tart, taste, treat, terse, tape, ten
V - vain, van, vast, vent, vest, veer
E - ear, erase, earnest, east, even, event, ever
A - art, ape, air, attain, ant, are, ain't, aster, arrest, apt, avert, aspen

PALINDROME (No letter may be used more than once.) page 14
P - pal, pale, poem, pail, pan, pad, pond, pine, pin, pole, pod, plan, plain, pain, plod, pare, pear, pore, prom, prime, prone
L - line, lime, lad, lop, lope, lamp, loam, lore, loan, lane, lend, liar, leap, lap, lame, lard, lair, land, lean, lead, led, lid, lip, learn
N - nail, nod, node, nor, nap, nape, near
D - dime, dare, dear, dial, dome, dole, drone, dram, damp, dope, doe, dam, dean, dream, dale, drape, drip, drop, dip, deal
R - roam, rail, rain, ran, rind, ram, ramp, read, rope, reap, ream, roe, real, rend, ripe, ripen, rip, rap, rid, ride
M - mine, mile, male, mail, man, men, mane, mad, made, mod, mode, modern, mole, moan, map, mope, mop, mean, mend, main, mare, mire, more, moral, morale
A - ape, aim, ail, ale, and, amp, air, ample, are
I - I'm, ire, ion, impale
O - one, ole, oar, ode, open, oral, opal
E - ear, earn, end, era

WORD BEHEADINGS   page 20

Beheading 1. trail, rail, ail, Al, a
Beheading 2. fight, gift, git, G.I.
Beheading 3. sauce, case, sac, AC, a

MORE WORD BEHEADINGS   page 21

Beheading 4. savior, savor, oars, S.A.R., as
Beheading 5. earth, thar, tar, at, T(shirt)
Beheading 6. lawyer, layer, real, ear, RA

TASTY SYLLABLES   page 28

1. beverage 2. hamburger 3. potato 4. cucumber 5. pineapple 6. broccoli
7. spaghetti 8. chocolate 9. sandwiches 10. vanilla 11. mayonnaise 12. barbecue
13. casserole 14. marmalade 15. strawberry

SYLLABLES   page 29

2. vacation 3. exercise 4. basketball 5. afternoon 6. creative 7. microscope
8. lemonade 9. conductor 10. divided 11. telephone 12. kangaroo 13. tomorrow 14. seventeen

SYLLABLE MATCH-UP   page 30

1. circle 2. danger 3. simple 4. bakery 5. vacation 6. begin 7. tomorrow 8. secret
9. candy 10. journey 11. allow 12. cabin 13. tunnel 14. pretend 15. bottom 16. decide
17. offer 18. able 19. arrive 20. farther

COMPOUND GAME   page 33

41 Examples: downcast, overcast, overwork, homework, footwork, woodwork, groundwork,
rainbow, playground, playback, background, backboard, blackboard, blackball, blacksmith, baseboard,
cupboard, washboard, cardboard, eyebrow, eyelash, backlash, blackmail, mailman, salesman,
policeman, locksmith, sailboat, railroad, bedroom, washroom, sunlight, limelight, limestone, touchstone, touchdown,
touchback, downtown, buttercup, butterfly, plywood

SPLIT COMPOUNDS 1   page 34

1. briefcase 2. airtight 3. newspaper 4. classroom 5. beforehand 6. homework
7. typewriter 8. greenhouse 9. sunshine 10. Anybody

SPLIT COMPOUNDS 2   page 35

1. everywhere 2. tightrope 3. heavyweight

SECRET CODES   page 40

I _____ AM A MAGNIFICENT HUMAN BEING!
                    (Write your name on the line above.)

CRYPTOGRAPHY   page 41

IF YOU THINK YOU CAN, OR IF YOU THINK YOU CAN'T, YOU ARE RIGHT.
THIS PICTURE IS A "PUN" (A PLAY ON WORDS).

CRYPTOGRAM   page 42

Circus Animals:
1. elephant 2. dog 3. horse 4. pony 5. seal 6. gorilla 7. lion 8. tiger 9. camel
10. leopard

The Pet Shop:
1. flea powder 2. cage 3. goldfish 4. puppy 5. pet food 6. bird seed 7. kitten
8. turtle 9. hamster 10. canary

The Soda Fountain:
1. milk shake 2. sundae 3. ice cream 4. lemonade 5. malt 6. root beer 7. banana split
8. hot chocolate 9. sherbet 10. pudding

CODES TO CRACK 1   page 44

Sports:
soccer, football, baseball, hockey, track, roller skating, tennis, gymnastics,
basketball, ice skating, jogging, volleyball, badminton

Food:
spaghetti, hamburger, sandwiches, tuna casserole, fried chicken, macaroni, potato
salad, pancakes, steak, chow mein, pork chops, turkey, French fries

Holidays:
Christmas, Hanukkah, Halloween, Thanksgiving, Labor Day, Easter, Mother's Day,
Fourth of July, Columbus Day, Father's Day, Memorial Day, Veterans Day,
New Year's Day

CODES TO CRACK 2   page 45

School:

teacher, student, learning center, spelling, arithmetic, reading, homework, principal, writing, classroom, science, library, study

Flowers:

honeysuckle, daisy, petunia, buttercup, stock, daffodil, zinnia, pansy, violet, iris, geranium, rose, poppy

Orchestra Instruments:

trumpet, violin, oboe, flute, trombone, bassoon, harp, piano, viola, French horn, cello, kettledrum, bass

A STRANGE MESSAGE   page 46

Fellow Colonists,   7 Draco 5097

The mother ship from ZOREX landed on earth last week (earth time) in Peru. OUR ONENESS visited the Yucatan and Egypt before moving the ship to its present location. It now awaits our gathering. Close your eyes and breathe deeply. Let our minds reveal the ship's location. OUR ONENESS will direct our way. Fear no human intervention; the ship is a fifth dimensional model, invisible to normal earth eyes. We may attend the gathering of minds in our earth forms or through astral projection. Those using nonhuman forms, or assigned to underwater lives will use astral powers.

Peace, One-of-Us

POSITION PUZZLES   page 48

I understand, man overboard, undercover agent, long underwear, easy on the eyes, I overate, dark circles under his eyes, going around in circles, high chair, flat tire, downtown, crossroads, sick in bed, mixed-up kid, running around the block, scrambled eggs

MORE POSITION PUZZLES   page 49

broken heart, up in arms, right in the middle of everything, head over heels in love, neon lights, reading between the lines, very interesting, a little misunderstanding between friends, an uphill fight, walking tall, time after time (or double time), touchdown, six feet under ground, six of one kind, half a dozen of another, take one before each meal, paradise, rising costs, one in a million, a sock in the eye, three degrees below zero

WORD OVAL   page 54

surf, surface, face, ace, cent, center, enter, terrace, err, race, east, Easter, aster, ere, real, alm, almost, most, tea, tear, ear, earth, art, thump, hum, hump, ump, pa, pair, air, airplane, plan, plane, planet, lane, net, to, toss (Ump is an abbreviation.)

ALPHABET SOUP 1   page 57

bicycle, extra, puppets, kickball, school, pencil, homework, crayons, teacher, fuzzy, bubbles, animal, telephone, nightmare, request, everyday, ski jump, elephant, circus, cheetah, firefly, cricket, fastastic, playing, candy

ALPHABET SOUP 2   page 58

beauty, forgive, harmony universe, wholeness, healthy, abundance, prosperity, rainbow, enjoyment, sparkle, agree, cheerful, confidence, amazing, happy, great, delightful, relaxation, peace, renew, positive, perfect, excitement, quietly

ANTONYMS   page 59

1. late 2. lose 3. whole 4. receive 5. outside 6. top 7. gain 8. shut
9. love 10. remember 11. pretty 12. sad 13. play 14. dull 15. sorrow 16. child
17. narrow 18. separate 19. clear 20. familiar 21. positive 22. reply 23. private
24. wealthy 25. damage 26. cool 27. safety 28. quiet

SYNONYM GAME   page 60

1. MONEY, cash, funds, wealth 2. SILENT, quiet, still, soundless 3. CHANGE, vary, alter, shift 4. ANTICIPATE, expect, hope for, await 5. SURE, certain, unmistakable, positive 6. SMALL, diminutive, little, limited 7. STRENGTH, vigor, vitality, force 8. INTELLIGENT, bright, quick-witted, keen 9. QUESTION, search, seek, inquire 10. LARGE, enormous, vast, immense 11. POSSIBLE, likely, credible, achievable 12. LOUD, noisy, uproarious, booming 13. QUICK, prompt, swift, fast 14. PREDICT, foretell, forecast, prophesy

COLORFUL SYNONYMS   page 61

1. red 2. blue 3. colorless 4. yellow 5. brown 6. color 7. white 8. purple
9. bright colors 10. black 11. green 12. gray 13. different colors 14. orange

HOMONYMS   page 62

1. plain 2. maid 3. hear 4. pane 5. haul 6. herd 7. bawl 8. sighs
9. weigh 10. pail 11. hoarse 12. stake 13. male 14. board 15. knight
16. allowed 17. seller 18. through 19. wood 20. sail 21. eight 22. passed
23. steel 24. whole 25. hour 26. grate 27. mane 28. patience 29. fowl
30. moan 31. chews 32. serial 33. reign, rein 34. rode, rowed 35. so, sew
36. site, sight 37. there, they're 38. scents, sense 39. preys, praise
40. rite, write, wright

CATEGORIZING   page 63

Fruits:
cantaloupe, tangerine, guava, nectarine, orange, apricot, banana, pineapple, grapefruit, mango, peach, watermelon
Vegetables:
green pepper, carrot, corn, turnip, asparagus, celery, cucumber, cabbage, spinach, broccoli, Brussels sprouts, cauliflower
Flowers:
daffodil, marigold, violet, gardenia, carnation, poinsettia, chrysanthemum, tulip, petunia, orchid, daisy, geranium

PEOPLE, PLACES & THINGS   page 64

People:
contractor, archeologist, engineer, jockey, landscaper, mechanic, professor, astronomer, student, pilot, actor, reporter, architect, counselor, electrician, data processor
Places:
theater, factory, clinic, laboratory, school, county, garden, racetrack, office, courtroom university, classroom, airport, observatory, auditorium, museum
Things:
license, computer, microscope, instruments, artifact, machinery, lecture, airplane, horse, contract, telescope, textbook, consultation, newspaper, investment, equipment

PARTS OF SPEECH   page 65

Nouns:
friend, beach, mountain, captain, reptile, money, microscope, planet, passenger, governor, music, plant, sunset, photograph, zoo
Adjectives:
excellent, free, creative, peaceful, joyful, happy, beautiful, newsworthy, valuable, brave, eager, curious, cheerful, delightful, soft
Verbs:
listen, finish, receive, prefer, draw, laugh, choose, learn, celebrate, enjoy, agree, renew, vibrate, relax, accept (plant)

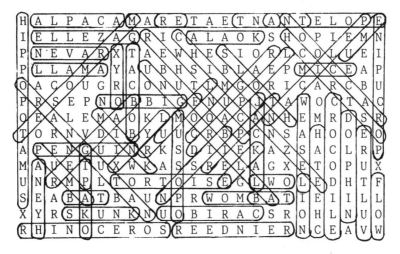

Twice: cow, deer, dog, fox, snake, tiger, whale

MORE ANIMALS   page 81

Other animals in this puzzle: ant, bat, lion, mare, mice, pig, owl

FIND THE ANIMALS   page 83

1. tiger 2. crocodile 3. dolphin 4. raccoon 5. chimpanzee 6. gazelle
7. hippopotamus 8. coyote 9. leopard 10. turkey 11. orangutan

HIDDEN ANIMALS   page 84

1. seal 2. bobcat 3. dolphin 4. camel 5. hawk 6. ape 7. llama 8. panther
1. caribou, crow 2. weasel, emu 3. leopard, ant 4. owl, rat 5. lion, bat 6. loon,
gorilla, and newt 7. bison, bear 8. sloth, beaver

CAMELEPHANT   page 86

2. rhinoceros, ostrich 3. panther, heron 4. turtle, leopard 5. ape, eel
6. kangaroo, rooster 7. goldfish, shark 8. ostrich, chimpanzee 9. cormorant,
anteater 10. antelope, pelican 11. constrictor, tortoise 12. zebra, rattler
Godzilla, llama; buffalo, Lorax; Hulk, kangaroo

MORE ANIMAL COMBINATIONS   page 87

Some possible answers: cardinalligator, hippopotamuskrat, cobrabbit, sealpaca, foxen,
alpacamel, cardinalpaca, camelk, giraferret, orioleopard, alligatoriole, badgerbil,
ostrichicken, antelopeacock, cowl, okapig, squirrelephant, squirrelk

SOME TEAM SPORTS

1. football
2. hockey
3. volleyball
4. soccer
5. baseball
6. softball
7. badminton

WATER SPORTS

1. rowing
2. surfing
3. fishing
4. swimming
5. diving
6. boating
7. water skiing
8. sailing
9. yachting

YOU CAN DO THESE SPORTS BY YOURSELF OR WITH OTHERS

1. skateboarding
2. golf
3. running
4. weight lifting
5. hiking
6. gymnastics
7. bowling
8. cycling
9. archery

OTHER SPORTS

1. racing
2. tennis
3. hunting
4. handball
5. boxing

TRACK & FIELD

1. cross-country
2. discus
3. hurdling
4. pole vaulting
5. javelin throwing

TEAM SPORTS

1. basketball
2. rugby
3. water polo
4. speedball
5. lacrosse

WITH ANIMALS

1. horseback riding
2. dog racing

ALWAYS OUTDOORS

1. mountain climbing
2. spelunking
3. lawn bowling

IN THE AIR

1. sky diving
2. hang gliding
3. hot air ballooning

WINTER SPORTS

1. skiing
2. ice skating
3. speed skating
4. ski jumping
5. snowmobiling
6. bobsledding

MORE SPORTS

1. jogging
2. wrestling
3. roller skating
4. tumbling
5. fencing
6. drag racing

GAMES PEOPLE PLAY   page 94

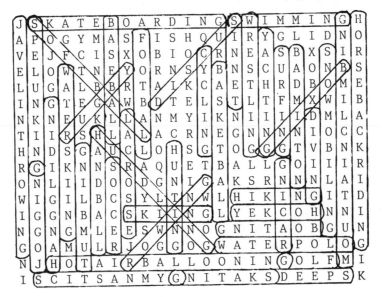

FOOD WORDS   page 98

hamburger, rice, ice, ham, ha, burger, urge, egg, eggplant, plant, plan, an, ant, taco, corn, acorn, or, nut, tomato, to, mat, at, tow, watermelon, water, melon, me, on, term, ate, onion, ion, strawberries, straw, berries, err, aw, raw, sherbet, she, he, her, herb, bet, yam, am, oranges, ran, rang, range, sham

SCRAMBLED FOOD   page 100

1. hamburger 2. French fries 3. spaghetti 4. broccoli 5. steak 6. baked potatoes
7. eggs 8. pork chops 9. bread 10. cheese 11. sweet potatoes 12. catsup
13. chicken 14. lemonade 15. apples 16. peanut butter 17. popcorn 18. hot dogs
19. ham 20. pizza 21. oranges 22. salad 23. ravioli 24. macaroni 25. milk
26. carrots 27. peaches 28. mustard 29. cookies 30. granola

INTERNATIONAL FOOD   page 102

AMERICAN - fried chicken, turkey and dressing, hot dogs, barbequed ribs, baked ham, steak, hamburgers

MEXICAN - burritos, enchiladas, quesadillas, tacos, tamales, tostadas, chile rellenos

ITALIAN - veal scallopini, lasagne, ravioli, eggplant parmigiana, turkey tetrazzini, cioppino

CHINESE - egg foo yong, won tons, sweet and sour pork, egg rolls, fried rice, stir fry, Peking duck

WHAT'S COOKING?   page 104

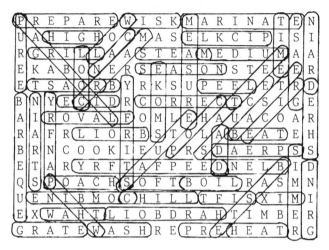

PLACES TO LIVE   page 106

1. house 2. trailer 3. condominium 4. mansion 5. wigwam 6. apartment 7. palace
8. farmhouse 9. igloo 10. cabin 11. ranch 12. flat 13. hut 14. recreational vehicle
15. castle 16. town house 17. A-frame 18. tract home 19. tepee (also spelled teepee)
20. duplex 21. cottage 22. shanty 23. hotel 24. shack 25. lodge 26. tent

HOME BUILDING SPECIALISTS   page 108

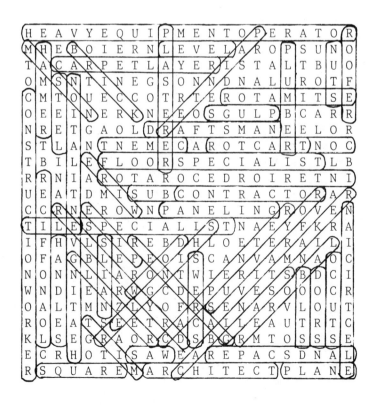

```
F R A N K E N S T E I N G H O U L S
A U H A U N T Y R A C S O O Z E S I
N O N I G H T D H O W L B R O O M M
T N A I G Z Y N R F E I L R L W O A
A U T N A G R A G R G T I O Z N S G
S E M U T S O C N E N H N R S P I I
Y P E R C G O I A A E S T E K R N N
G O R P A N I C N K R R E L K E E A
R G O U A P P L E S T R L A M O T T
O O K E I R H S T G S P O O K A N I
T R I K S A M G H O S T S K E E A O
E D R A C U L A G H A R V E S T L N
S L I M E L A P I W A R L O C K O W
Q U E E R I E W R E M A E R C S K I
U W E R E W O L F U L L M O O N C T
E O P A R T I E S N I K P M U P A C
T R I C K O R T R E A T C A T S J H
```

CHRISTMAS WORD TREE   page 119

Christmas, Christ, as, mast, street, tree, to, torn, or, ornament, name, am, amen, men, car, me, cards, stockings, stock, tock, in, king, Santa, ant, an, tag, gift, if, mist, is, mistletoe, let, toe, gather, gathering, he, the, her, at, ring, glove, love, lo, oven, enjoy, joy

WORDS FROM THE HEART   page 121

valentines, vale, ale, tine, lent, tin, in, sat, at, is, satisfaction, fact, act, action, ion, on, remark, remarkable, mark, ma, ark, able, lever, ever, eve, every, very, everything, thing, thin, great, eat, thought, ought, ugh, thou

SPACE FLIGHT   page 124

```
S P A C E S H U T T L E F L I G H T M P C
C O U N D F O V O Y A G E R N O Y U A I O
I R X F O F U R U T I N G I E U P A N L M
E E I F C O S E C O N F D A T A E N N O M
N D L O K T T H Y M N F T I B R O E T D U
T N I E I S O U D E A W T O Y A S R T O N
I A E S N A N P O L N C G T I O T S S C I
F M R A G L E M W A N O M E A F N S P K C
I Y T A B C O N T R O L S G R I A A C E A
C O P H Y S I C A L E X A M S A C L C E T
R C O U N T D O W N A I B M U L O C E H I
E O W S H I E L D P I H S E C A P S F Y O
S J E T T I S O N T I G N I T I O N L Y N
E G R O U N D C R E W A L C O C K P I T S
A N U A P O L L O K N W O D L O O C G E E
R A N O E L A U N C H S I T E K C U H F L
C S I A L O R T N O C N O I S S I M T A I
H A T M O S P H E R E E T I L L E T A S T
```

WEATHER ANAGRAMS   page 125

1. warm 2. cold 3. hot 4. hail 5. cool 6. sunshine 7. thunder 8. lightning
9. downpour 10. stormy 11. drizzle 12. cloudy 13. chilly 14. snow 15. snowstorm
16. sleet 17. gusty 18. foggy 19. windy 20. rainy 21. icy 22. humid 23. balmy
24. freezing 25. cyclone 26. overcast 27. tornado 28. hurricane 29. typhoon
30. forecast 31. blizzard 32. front 33. report 34. rainstorm

HINK PINKS   page 127

Hink Pinks: fat cat, Swiss miss, big wig, glad dad, cross boss, small ball, big pig, wet pet, blue pew
Hinky Pinkies: fatter platter, phony pony, higher fire, lazy daisy (silly lily, etc.), crystal pistol, sloppy copy, butter cutter
Hinkety Pinketies: annual manual

FOREIGN LANGUAGES   page 128

```
P O R T U G U E S E R B O C R O A T I A N
U K D A N I S H Z C B U L G A R I A N I A
N E N G L I S H H E B R E W U T N A B O I
J A R A B I C A I E F M G E R M A N N A D
A N S L O V A K C S I E K L G A E L I C O
B I P O L I S H I M N S O S P A N I S H B
I T A G T H A I D A N E R H C N E R F U M
N A I G E W R O N G I Z E N A I S R E P A
H L A O T I A N A I S K A S U A H C E Z C
S H S I K R U T L N H G N R O M A N I A N
I V I E T N A M E S E S E N I H C Z E C H
D N A I S S U R C J A P A N E S E S I R I
D A U K R A I N I A N U A I L I H A W S N
I I T A L I A N M A G Y A R G H M O N G A D
Y N A O M I K S E I R I S A N S K R I T U
H A W A I I A N R U S S I R I S H C T U D
A M H A R I C U L U Z R N O G N I D N A M
S W E D I S H A S H A N T I S F U L A H A
```

137